ERNATIONAL ICAL THOUGHT OF , NEHRU AND LOHIA

NALIN ANADKAT

BHARATIYA KALA PRAKASHAN

DELHI-INDIA

Published by :
C.P. Gautam
Bharatiya Kala Prakashan
3421-A, IInd Floor,
Narang Colony,
Tri Nagar, Delhi-110035
Ph. 7153083

First Published : 2000

ISBN : 81-86050-45-0

Laser Typesetting by :
Ishan Comprint
Gurgaon (Haryana)

Printed at :
Santosh Offset Press
Inder Lok, Delhi-110035

Dedicated to

Shri Rameshbhai (Sheelubhai) Bhimajiyani

and

Smt. Rupa Bhimajiyani

FOREWORD

It is quite a challenging academic task to provide a conceptual framework to the international political thought of Gandhi Nehru and Lohia as they were basically men of action. Gandhi, Nehru and Lohia played a very vital role not only in liberating India from the clutches of foreign rule but while doing so they had a vision of a new world order free from all forms exploitation and dominacne. Dr. Nalin Anadkat in his book makes a seminal contribution to the literature of International relations not merely by analyzing the motivating thought of Gandhi, Nehru and Lohia but he encapsulates their ideas about a more stable, equitable and peaceful world at large in his book.

As the author has rightly admitted in his introductory chapter that none of the three (Gandhi, Nehru and Lohia) were either philosophers or theoreticians and therefore to find any thematic consistency in their ideas is unthinkable. It is for this reason Dr. Anadkat's work deserves attention as he had to go back to the roots where tradition of thinking on problematic of world-order, peace and justice was laid by the great western political thinkers like Hobbes, Grotious and Kant.

There may be an element of truth when allegations are made that there is no tradition of conceptual thinking in India. The fact of the matter is that in Indian contest it is from praxis to theory, which was a challenge for the scholar. Not that our men of action had no foundation of normative thinking but they did not systemize it or theorize it. It is this vacuum which scholars like Dr. Anadkat has tried to fill though his work.

While theorizing about Gandhi, Nehru and Lohia the author very emphatically makes it clear that the concern of peace and order has been perennial as the pendulam of war and peace has never been absent in international society. The author has conceptualized international society within which he has situated the concept of order as done by the Western scholars. Dr. Anadkat has shown as to how Gandhi, Nehru and Lohia were not far from the realistic notion of the causes of war and peace—though they did not provide any thoretical foundation to their concern.

In this book Dr. Anadkat has succeeded in integrating the western conceptual model of peace and order with the thinking of Gandhi, Nehru and Lohia and in the process he proves the relevance of universality in matters of war and peace.

Gandhi who, while he walked an untrodden path, spoke about his macro-vision of life, not only for India but also for the whole world. Gandhi had the unique distinction of combining resistance with a constructive vision for the future. For him India's struggle for freedom was to be visualized in the context of the world. He knew that when India would be free, no other country would remain in bondage. Gandhi was neither the first nor the last of those leaders who, while waging the struggle for freedom, laid down their ideas about the shape of the new world that they had envisaged for the future.

But, rather than delineating the emerging thoughts of many of them, the author has judiciously selected three of them, namely, Gandhi (1869-1948), Nehru (1889-1964) and Lohia (1910-1967) all of them expressing their views and ideas about the world they saw around them. Though contemporary of each other and fighting together in the struggle of freedom, they belonged to different age groups. All three of them had first hand knowledge of western society and had the opportunity of developing their own world views. Deeply aware and sensitized by their experience of foreign domination, these leaders were not unaware of the prevalent practices and operations of the international world—a world that was highly Euro-centric, the remaining areas of the world being peripheral in support of the dominant world order. Such an order was, in essence, anarchical with a modicum of system that came about as result of the Treaty of Westphalia (148) and functioned largely to the advantage of the dominant powers of the world.

Under such a system there was little chance for peace, order, fair play and justice. The system vacillated between peace and war, between order and disorder. The nation states observed a semblance of order because it is in their self-interest and mutual advantage.

If free India were to project itself in such a world and participate in it what kind of world would it be? How would it be organized, if at all? What kind of world order would India aim at? How could global peace and order be ensured in the world?

Gandhi's eclectic vision embraced the whole world in a highly humanistic fashion where every individual and nation was to be an integral part of the whole and live in peace, in a spirit of dignified interdependence. Since greed and injustice were the root cause of the wars a new equitable order was to emerge where society and people would count for more than the state or Government. Gandhi had unbounded faith in the unity of humankind and believed in co-operation and harmony rather than in conflict and confrontation as the prime nature of the universe and society. If world federation were to be formed, it would place justice before order, accept the rich diversity of the world and be ready to resolve conflicts in a peaceful manner. The United Nations could hardly fit in such a world order chiefly because it was based upon the interests of the powerful that militated against the equality of all the nations.

Following the footsteps of Gandhi, Nehru had great abhorrence for imperialism, racialism and exploitation. He stood for rational nationalism. For him nationalism was a good servant but a bad master. He realized the growing trend towards interdependence and stood for a union of fee nations. Having a sense of history he welcomed an Eastern Westphalia as a full-fledged extension of the European Westphalia (1648).

Nehru abjured power politics and favoured democratization of international politics composed of free and equl nation-states. Nehru's strategy of change involved search for a new paradigm that would strengthen temper of peace based upon mutual tolerance, co-operation and equal opportunity of all. Prevalence of fear and lack of democratic process were the main reasons behind war. He championed the five principles of Panchsheel for furtherance of this ideal. Nehru wanted India to be a meeting ground, a confluence of democracy and socialism. Like Gandhi he stood for creating a new man, a new leadership and a new equitable world order. By championing the philosophy of scientific humanism he aspired to combine intuition of the East with the science of the West.

Taking his clue from Gandhi and Nehru, Lohia stands for a more positive and ambitious programme for ensuring global order and peace. Three-monster viz. Hunger, slavery and war beguile the world according to him. Their eradication would need modification of the way the world is stratified into hegemonic versus peripheral powers. The supreme need of the hour is to ensure human development, what Lohia terms as "approximation", to a desirable standard of life. For the realization of the goal, Lohia suggests a programme to be initiated by rich nations. He wants participation of several political parties, creation of a World

Development Authority and a creative role of Non Governmental Organizations of World in bringing about the change. In order to realize this goal Lohia wants to recourse to the technique of Satyagraha at the international level.

This book is an outstanding contribution to the field of international relations because through his work Dr. Anadkat indicates the notion of "VASUDHAIV KUTUMBAKAM" (global family) by using analytical tools in a much wider perspective.

Peace Research Centre
Gujarat Vidhyapith
Ahmedabad-380014
Gujarat.

Prof. Devavrat N. Pathak
Former vice Chancellor,
Saurashtra University,
Gujarat.

ACKNOWLEDGEMENTS

The idea to pursue a research on the international dimension of the thinking of Gandhi, Nehru and Lohia had emerged in the early 1990s, from the discussion I had with my colleagues in the department of Political Science, M.S. University of Baroda. The long discussion with Dr. H.C. Shukul, Dr. Kanti Bajpai and Shri Shivanand Patnaik helped me to shape my ideas. In view of fruition of my study in form of a book, I express my deep gratitude to former professor and head, Dr. A.P. Rana, professor Thomas Pantham, professor V.G. Nandedkar and professor D.H. Mohite of the department of Political Science for their institutional support and help.

I am very grateful to the various librarians for helping me locating resources in their libraries. I would like to express my special thanks to the librarians of Jawaharlal Nehru University and Nehru Memorial libraries of New Delhi, Gandhi memorial library of Mumbai and the librarians of the Bombay University as well as the U.S.I.S. library of Bombay. I gratefully acknowledge the help I received from Smt. Mrinal Gore Smarak Trust library, Goregaon, specially for the materials on Ram Manohar Lohia. I would like to specially mention American Studies Research Center (ASRC), Hyderabad; and above all Shreemati Hansa Mehta library of the M.S. University of Baroda, Vadodara.

I am especially grateful to the Ford Foundation programme extended to my Department as I generously used its research grant for fieldwork to collect data and primary source material for this work. The major credit goes to the Ford Foundation for the publication of this work, as without its institutional and financial support, it would have been very difficult to visit various libraries in India.

How can I miss to thank Mr. Dinubhai and Mrs. Nandiniben Karia, my hosts at Mumbai, whose warm and affectionate hospitality at their house on the scenic and enchanting Arabian Sea shore helped me a lot in conceptualization of ideas of my study. My frequent visit to Mumbai never shook their patience and affection.

Dr. Manoj Soni and Dr. J.K. Khan my colleagues in the departments of Political Science and English respectively in the Sardar Patel University, to whom I owe a great deal for their consummate editorial skill to lend lucidity to this work.

Last but not the least, my family, specially Mini—my wife, Ruchi—my daughter, my sons—Samir and Alok, deserve mention for their forbearance and patience in putting up with my unavoidable ordeal for completing this work.

Nalin Anadkat

CONTENTS

INTRODUCTION

Mohandas Gandhi, Jawaharlal Nehru and Ram Manohar Lohia were neither philosophers, theorists nor system builders. All of them were men of action. As a matter of fact, action of any kind is never possible until a theory of some kind is presupposed, truly or falsely. For each of them, actively associated with the struggle for Indian independence, politics was an art realized in action, not a science insisting upon a theory to ground action. Each of them possessed a great and biding intuitional insight into the nature of Indian and international reality, which is valid even today. It is, therefore, impossible to deny that they had any contribution in shaping the tradition of Science of Politics. The main hypothesis of this study is that hitherto an international dimension of their political thinking is neglected. It is presumed here that their reference to the international dimension of the nation-state is not peripheral to their thought system. They have thought deeply and expressed extensively, either orally or through their writings, on the problematic of 'global order and peace' within the parameter of the nation-state system. To date, no academic study in India has attempted to reconstruct their thinking into a theoretical framework which would consolidate the notion of international society. This study is a modest attempt to explore that direction through research. Their ideas are available piecemeal-scattered over their writings and actions. To understand these and derive concepts out of them, these need to be assembled, assimilated and analysed and the undercurrent need to be discovered. This involves penetrating them beyond the obvious concerns of their programme of action and uncovering the analytical foundations on which they were based. Only this way we can hopefully infer the rationale of how they wanted to tackle the contending problems of global order and peace.

The concept and analysis evolving out of the thinking of these political celebrities require to be translated into the vocabulary of contemporary literature. They also need to be related to the conceptual analytical framework of Western thinkers in order to ascertain non-

Western, or especially Indian, thinking on peace. Hence, the thinking of Gandhi, Nehru and Lohia is scrutinized within the theoretical framework evolved by the Western thinkers: Thomas Hobbes, Immanuel Kant and Hugo Grotius.

Theoretically, the fundamental question of all social sciences has remained the same, which is, the creation of a good life. The corpus of 'International Order' theorizing is very much concerned with the substantive goal of creating conditions for good life for individual human beings. The main thrust of this study is to analyse the nature of international order, both in terms of theoretical accounts of its working and the historical examination of its operational principles. However, the focus will continuously be upon the nature of international order and its potential for reform and how Gandhi, Nehru, and Lohia view it.

The central problem of the world order is related with the causes of war and the conditions of peace. The causes of war are undoubtedly many and diverse, but the real problem is how to think about war and peace, knowing fully well that the nature of our analysis itself may significantly affect the conclusion of this inquiry. This study, therefore, relate that problem to the nature of international society which Gandhi, Nehru and Lohia had intuitively conceived. It also considers how the world order is maintained or ought to be maintained, not only for the survival of the nation-states, but to promote the "common good" of the mankind on the globe.

These political leaders were significantly active on national and international scene for a considerable time. The prime period of their lives were spent fighting against the British Rule, manifesting 'the mightiest empire' and 'the Great Power' of their times. They were successful even to cause the decline of the British Empire as India's independence had set the ball rolling for the decolonization process throughout Asia and Africa. Mainly during their active political lives, the two world-wars occured and the two major international organizations, namely, the League of Nations and the United Nations Organization emerged to create an alternative world order and peace. They were, thus, witness to many important international events which changed the map of the world and the destiny of millions of people.

The trio of Gandhi, Nehru and Lohia was educated in European universities. Consequently, they fell under the influence of many world famous writers and scholars and statesmen. While fighting against the British Raj, at home, they took out their own News Papers in order to circulate their reflections on those international events, which caused great and far-fetching effect on the history of international relations. The rise of Asian power - Japan (1905), the victory of the Communism in Russia (1917) and in China (1948); the rise and fall of Fascism and Nazism in Germany and Italy; the inhuman aspect of Fascism; the massacre of Jews in Germany; the rape of Czechoslovakia; the impotence of England and France against ghastly and cowardly acts of Hitler—all these affected each of them and each had a sharp reaction to those events. To date, no adequate attention has been paid to the international dimension of their thought. Infact, the main stream of their thinking was geared towards global order and peace.

No academic study in India attempts to reconstruct this contribution and identify it as a distinctively Indian contribution to the area of peace studies. This study is an exploratory attempt to signify the contribution of these leaders by bridging a critical gap, however, tentatively, in the Indian contribution to International Relations Studies in general and Peace Research in particular.

Substantively, all the three leaders showed the manner in which it might be possible to "think globally and act locally" and "to see the 'macrocosm' in the 'microcosm'. They always viewed Indian national struggle for independence as a part of the international movement against imperialism and a movement towards the creation of a just global society. They never viewed India's struggle for freedom in isolation but as a part of the world movement for freedom and equality and for democratizing the international society, then dominated by the imperial powers, viz., England and France.

Gandhi, Nehru and Lohia, in their speeches and writing, have nevertheless, reacted to the international events of their times but basically they were addressing the basic issues of "state" and "society" from international point of view. They were aware of international order within which they were operating. They also knew which agency would maintain international order and so, were determined to improve it, and if needed, even uproot the prevailing unjust and dominant international order.

This study, therefore, is an attempt to work out a perspective evolved by Gandhi, Nehru and Lohia individually regarding the nature and functioning of international society. The problematic of order and peace is always concerned with the nature and functioning of the international society. Hence this study raises some fundamental questions regarding international society and tries to obtain relevant answers from the thinking of Gandhi, Nehru and Lohia. The most fundamental question in the study of international relations is, 'what is meant by international society?' and 'how it operates according to Gandhi, Nehru and Lohia?'

The second question addresses the views of Gandhi, Nehru and Lohia on the existing order which is the outcome of the nature of international society. Order, however, can not exist in the absence of 'society,' for the latter provide the essential normative framework for relations of any regularity and certainly of the least complexity. The question regarding international order is addressed to three of them to ascertain whether the existing order is viewed by them as progressive or regressive? Progress means irreversible ameliorative change in the existing order. If they were dissatisfied with the operation of the nation-state system, what type of systemic change they would suggest? Would they really suggest any improvement in the existing international order (or disorder)? What were the main reasons they would have analysed for (dis)order in international society? Finally, this study attempts to find out, whether they suggest any new approach or strategy (which we may call distinctly Indian) to transform the existing "society of state" (international order) into a "society of mankind" (world order)? In other words, this theoretical inquiry addresses their position as regards to: (1) system maintenance? (2) system change?; or (3) system transformation?

The above theoretical questions are addressed to Gandhi, Nehru and Lohia with a view to finding out what is their conception of "common good," or a "good life" in a global society.

National Society and International Society

There is a dichotomy between politics in domestic society and that in "international society." The main distinguishing factor between the two is their "ends" and the "units" which participate in politics. The end (aim) of participating in politics in international society is basically to survive as a sovereign unit. It is not the people who directly participate in international politics. It is through the unit (actor), i.e., is the 'state'. It is on the basis of this criterion that a distinction is often made between national politics or domestic politics on the one hand and international politics on the other. The methods prohibited in international politics are fewer than those prohibited in national politics. Methods like direct violence, fraud, and corruption are prohibited by municipal law in national politics. But in case of international politics, war has been permissible in one sense or another as a natural instrument of foreign policy.

Secondly the national law is the basis of national policies, while the basis of international politics is the international law. The national law as a general rule has been more comprehensive and much more effectively enforceable than the international law. Thus, national politics has a greater basis of order and a greater degree of regularity than international politics. In international society, one sovereign state threatens another state and all the states function under constant threat. On the contrary, the threat in national politics is not directly to the survival of a state. The threat is experienced by a group of people who hold power within the state from another group of people who aspire to capture power.

The modes of operation in national society and international society are different. National or domestic society politics is conceived in terms of persuasion, peaceful legislation and administration, and periodic elections especially in democratic countries. In international society, politics deals with sharp ends of power politics i.e. 'use of force,' and 'the threat to use force.' In this sense, international politics and national politics operate at different levels involving different issues, different goals, and different interests. (The main distinguishing factors are borrowed from a theoretical book written by Mahendra Kumar (ed., 1994) entitled 'Non-violence: Contemporary Issues and Challenges, Gandhi Peace Foundation, New Delhi.') In fact, much of the distinction between domestic and international politics, whether in their subject matter or in the mode of their operation arises from the fundamental reality that within a nation there exists an effective central authority (government) while no effective government operates over nations (Hadley Bull, Anarchical Society).

A domestic society connotes to "civil society" and an "international society" is an embodiment of "state of nature" (of Hobbes). The basic value of a domestic society is to achieve "good life" and there prevails a consensus on the concept of "good life." In an international society, the basic problem is that of survival of a state. Hence, an international society constantly experiences tension towards achieving the goal of "good life". Western scholars like Hobbes, Kant and Grotius have tried to address this tension in their own way. In the last chapter of this book, an attempt has been made to find out how this problematic (good life) is addressed by Gandhi, Nehru and Lohia in order to resolve this enigmatic tension. Theoretically, the most fundamental question of all social sciences has remained the same, which is the creation of good life on this planet.

The international dimensions of the thought of Gandhi, Nehru and Lohia are not examined in isolation. They are viewed, examined, categorized and related to dominant schools of thought conceptualized as 'Realism', 'Rationalism' and 'Revolutionism'. They are associated, hence, respectively with the view points of Thomas Hobbes (1588-1679), Hugo Grotius (1583-1645), and Immanuel Kant (1724-1804). The conceptualization of international society by each of them, more or less, captures the reality of international relations. They were among the first few western thinkers who coherently thought on the issue of international relations and their line of thinking developed and got identified with schools of realism, rationalism and revolutionism respectively. Many other thinkers, later on, interpreted and re-interpreted their views on the reality of international relations. They became well-known neo-realists, neo-Grotian and neo-Kantian. The views of Gandhi, Nehru and Lohia are considered in relation to these established view points. Thus, this study is an attempt to continue this great theoretical discourse on the problematic of international relations by assimilating discourses of Gandhi, Nehru and Lohia.

I, as a researcher, acknowledge that the three schools of thought are not exhaustive and exclusive. It is also accepted that many eminent writers and historical personalities do not fit comfortably into any trend or tradition. Inspite of these limitations, the categories of Hobbes, Kant and Grotius are preferred mainly because they provide useful insights into many of the fundamental issues in international relations. The classical categories of inquiry, when applied to the international dimension of the thoughts of Gandhi, Nehru and Lohia offer they important insights into the nature and functioning of international society. The preliminary readings of, and on, Gandhi, Nehru and Lohia convincingly proves that, apart from being activists, they were visionary thinkers who in their vision of the world, could stand apart from the common place assumptions of their times. They could conceive alternatives to established ways of doing things in the field of international relations. They urged their contemporaries to move forward in the direction of new and better goals and also suggested, to some extent, practiced means by which those goals may be achieved.

The Chapterization

This study is divided into five chapters: Chapter 1: Theoretical Framework; Chapter 2: Gandhi's Conception of International Society; Chapter 3: Nehru's Conception of International Society; Chapter 4:

Lohia's Conception of International Society; and Chapter 5 Conclusion.

The first chapter defines and codifies three dominant schools of thought in the light of the conception of international society. They are categorized as Realist, Rationalist, and Revolutionary. These western schools of thought are represented chiefly by Hobbes and Machiavelli, Hugo Grotius and Kant. Their views are further divided into two subcategories:

(i) Functioning of the International Society: Organizing and Operational Principles of International Society, and

(ii) Strategy suggested (or not suggested) for transforming international society while ascertaining their views on "good life".

The second, third and fourth chapters discuss the views of Gandhi, Nehru and Lohia respectively, keeping in view, the theoretical categories and sub-categories outlined in the first chapter. These chapters conceptualize views of these thinkers on the reality of international relations as experienced and reacted to by each of them. Thus, these chapters are structured within the framework of the first chapter. In the concluding chapter, an effort has been made to focus on a comparative framework, their differences from the western thinkers (Hobbes, Kant and Grotius) so that uniqueness of Indian thinking on the problematic of global order and peace may be ascertained. In other words, the originality of the proposed research rests on encapsulating three trends of Indian political activists, viz., Gandhi, Nehru and Lohia within the broad spectrum of international relations. In a modest way, the study may be termed as original as far as the comparative perspective of western and Indian thinking is concerned with regard to International Relations.

Methodology

The subject matter of on empirical study is a matter of experience and observation. It is based on the findings of a researcher. It may propound a theory related with the phenomena observed and studied. The problem of methodology arises specially in an empirical study. An empirical research is, as such, interested in studying a particular phenomenon, viz., International Terrorism. On studying it, a researcher may evolve an empirical theory out of the findings. However, the present study falls in a category of classical tradition of International Relations Studies.

The classical theory connotes to the tradition of speculation about the 'relations between states' and about the 'society of states'. According to Martin Wight, the most fundamental question one raises in international theory is 'what is international society?'

Moreover, the classical approach theorizes from philosophy, history and law and it is built on the normative concerns. The classical theory mainly concerns itself, with what R.H. Jackson refers to, as theory about 'good life'. The classical theory differs from the empirical theory mainly on the ground that it makes, descriptive and explanatory statements about the structure, units, processes of international politics transcending time, location, and personality and it does not neglect the normative concerns.

The scholars who are working in the classical tradition define the problematic in terms of the causes of war and the conditions of peace, security, or order. States are regarded as essential actors and, hence, essential units of analysis, while the dominant image of the world is a system of sovereign states, characterized by international anarchy or the absence of centralized authority.

This study attempts to study thoughts of Gandhi, Nehru and Lohia within the classical tradition. The dominant paradigm revolves around three basic notions: (i) states recognize no higher authority; (ii) states live in a state of nature; and (iii) resulting security dilemma forces them to continue to live in a state of nature. The thought of Gandhi, Nehru and Lohia are scrutinized within this parameter. Hence, the problem of methodology (as being understood in a traditional sense: quantitative or qualitative) does not arise.

This study, nevertheless, is a library study but not at all an arm chair one, churning out material based on historical narration. It is not a descriptive study, but an indepth analytical and prescriptive one. Methodologically, the study is within the construct of the subject matter, viz., two schools representating the Western and the Eastern thinking. The Eastern thinking is basically constructed on 'the concepts derived by intuition,' not necessarily on 'intellection'. Modern science prefers "concepts by intellection," to "the concepts by intuition." It makes increasing use of the concept by intellection, whereas art, music, religion, aesthetics make increasing use of concepts by intuition. For example, there is a basic difference between *SATYA* (truth) a concept by intuition and truth, a concept of intellection. The former is derived basically from the Eastern thinking and it is liable to direct verification of its practioner. While the latter is an empirical 'truth' of modern science and it is open only to indirect verification for confirmation. Thus, it creates a dilemma as to how to study the ideas of Gandhi, Nehru and

Lohia on international relations, as one has to face two different ontological and epistomological positions. One faces such dilemma in cases when concepts are converted by a thinker for his purpose. For instance, Gandhi, no doubt, accepts certain concepts from the Western thinkers like Tolstoy, Thoreau and Ruskin, but he converts them to their equivalents in terms of concepts by intuition to fit them within his own system. Similarly, Nehru's concept of "Panchsheel", derived from Buddhist tradition is applied to conducting bilateral relations between two nations in international relations.

In order to solve the problem of epistemology, the study, therefore, takes the views of the 'realist', 'revolutionary' and 'rational' schools of thinking as the base in the light of which the thinking of Gandhi, Nehru and Lohia are studied. It also relates their concepts to the nature of international society. In the concluding chapter, the positions of Gandhi, Nehru and Lohia are scrutinized in order to ascertain as to how far their intuition-based concepts result into intellectual orientation. The purpose of this study is not merely to deal with conversion, but to find out in what way India's contribution to the cosmos of international relations in the field of peace research is unique.

Sources

The primary source material is the writings of the thinkers themselves. All the three of them were prolific writers as they were educated in the Western universities. Especially, Dr. Rammanohar Lohia had even obtained his Ph.D. degree from a German University. Autobiography and biographies of Gandhi and Nehru respectively are also considered. The Gandhian and Nehruvian institutes have published anthology of their writings on international relations, which have also been incorporated in the analysis.

The secondary source material on their works (writings) is not adequately available, except a few articles. No adequate attention has been paid to the international dimension of their thoughts. The study is, therefore, much constrained for want of adequate material.

Eventually, the introduction may be summed up with due clarification of the concepts considered in this study, viz., 'Order;' 'International Order;' World Order;' 'System'; and 'Society'.

Order

The concept of 'order' in the literature of International Relations Studies is a complex term. It is always understood as an antonym of 'disorder'. Thus, it has clear implication of enforcement of law. Hence, in the term 'law and order' it goes together with law. It has thus a legal implication. 'Order' is an asset to a society as it brings 'stability' in its domestic and social spheres. The domestic society is a civil society, which is governed by laws of the land. Order in that context, thus, connotes to the centralized authority. The concept of order in the literature of international relations is used inter-changeably, sometimes as 'international order' and sometimes as 'world order'. In the literature on 'world order', it becomes more dynamic concept as it envisages change on a much larger scale in international relations. It becomes a movement for a just world order and 'order' becomes a value-laden terminology.

Especially in this study, the concept of order has been taken both as a 'process' and as a 'substance'. Order in the sense of 'process' means formal in character. It emphasizes 'means' rather than 'ends'. Order in the sense of 'substance' means it is not enough to do things in order (in a systematic way). What is done should be such as to merit the word orderly. Thus, the concept of order does not refer to any stratified or systematic arrangement. This thesis presumes that there is some sort of order in the existing nation-state system which is referred to as international order. There is no world order as the international society is not yet composed of humanity as a unified family of man. International order simply refers to the fact that the states (nations) co-operate or inter-act and produce a situation in international relations. This is a prescriptive conception which involves value preference as order itself. Defining 'order' in precise terms would limit the inherent flexibility of the concept of order. The purpose in this thesis is to examine various modes of order as perceived by Gandhi, Nehru and Lohia. And to put it somewhat paradoxically, the fact remains that it is the prevailing state of disorder which stimulates great minds to think of order—thus the concept of order is within the framework of causation—every action good or bad has its cause and effects and order—disorder is no exception.

According to Hoffman, 'Order' has five meanings in the literature of International Relations. Two of them are purely descriptive, viz., Order as any arrangement of reality; and Order as the relation between the parts; two are analytical - partly descriptive and partly normative, viz., order as the minimum condition for existence, and order as the minimum condition for co-existence. The fifth meaning is purely normative, that is order as the condition for good life. This work takes into account the descriptive as well as prescriptive meanings of 'order', but eventually attempts to conceptualize the perspectives of Gandhi, Nehru and Lohia in the light of the fifth and the last conception of order.

International Order

This term refers to nation-state system. The states (about 185 as of today) are sole participator, and are independent, territorially limited and politically organized in international relations. They have their own governments (majority of them are non-democratic) and they inter-act among themselves. These states (not the people) are involved in conflicts as well as in co-operation. The people who reside within the territory of a state are considered 'citizens' of that state and they have rights and duties within the state only. These rights and duties are not trans-national. Their citizenship is confined only to the state to which they belong and to which they adhere their objectives. Nations pursue their respective national interests by peaceful means (diplomacy) or by resorting to a coercive methods. (in overt or covert manner - warfare). They build up their national power by organizing their coercive resources. States are interested more in 'security' than in 'peace'. Some authors believe that states provide the basis of the prevailing pattern of international society. According to Hedley Bull, sovereign states create international order and their discontinuity might destroy the stability of the international system as a whole.

The World Order

The concept of 'World Order' is different from that of 'International Order'. World order refers to the human society as a whole. This analytical category does not differentiate 'man' amongst citizens. It stands for order in the human society as a whole. It is a wider concept than order amongst sovereign states. It refers to the different principles of organization. The world order exponents deal with the issues and problems of global security and not with those of national security. The final goal is to achieve "human unity" based on the dignity of individual human being. It stands for 'global village'. The world order is 'human-centric' and not 'state-centric'. The 'World Order' is more fundamental than 'International Order' and morally it is prior to international order.

International System and Society

According to Hedley Bull, "A system of states (or international system) is formed when two or more states have sufficient contact between them, and have sufficient impact on one another's decisions, to cause them to behave - at least in some measure - as parts of a whole. A society of states (or international society) exists when a group of states (already forming a system) conscious of certain common interests and common values, form a society in the sense that they conceive themselves to be bound by a common set of rules in their relations with one another, and share in the working of common institutions."

Lastly, this work does not intend to undertake indepth study of the views of Thomas Hobbes, Immanuel Kant or Grotius, but only to construct a framework of analysis out of their views which impinges upon the aspect of international relations. The main focus is on the views of Gandhi, Nehru and Lohia. Their views are studied within the above framework.

Chapter 1

FRAMEWORK OF ANALYSIS : ALTERNATIVE CONCEPTIONS OF INTERNATIONAL SOCIETY

This chapter provides a framework of analysis on which the subsequent chapters are structured. In this chapter the basic theoretical question asked and answered is whether there is an international society? In response to this query, three coherent pattern. of thought have emerged in the discipline of international relations studies. The three categories identified are realism, rationalism, and revolutioalism. They are associated respectively with the thought of Thomas Hobbes, Hugo Grotius and Immanuel Kant. They agree on the answer that there is an international society but disagree on the nature and functioning of that society. The main distinguishing feature among them is the position adopted on 'international society'. The realist (or Hobbesian and Machiavellian) conception form one extreme and denies the existence of an effective international society. This school emphasises that 'society' can only be established by contract, and maintains that international relations is in a pre-contractual state of nature.

Revolutionism or Kantianism lies at the other extreme and posits that the existing community of states is 'unreal' - a complex of legal fictions and obsolescent diplomatic forms which conceals, obstructs and oppresses the real society of individual men and women. Thus, this school of thought identifies 'individual' and not 'states' as true members of the international society. This tradition conceives the present order composed of sovereign states, as illegitimate and believes that it will be inevitably replaced by order composed of mankind. Thus the Kantian tradition (the revolutionist) acknowledges society, but considers it to be illegitimate and temporary in nature.

Between these two categories lies the third, rationalism or Grotianism. This tradition rejects both the realist's claim that international society is a fiction and the revolutionist's assessment of the illegitimate and transitory nature of the states system. This tradition (Grotian) maintains that international politics is taking place within an international society composed of sovereign states. They are bound by natural laws. Hence international society is not anarchical as the natural law forms the basis of international society and the foundation for individual rights and responsibilities. Hence, Grotius rejected the replacement of the present system of sovereign states with world government on the ground that it would be too large, inefficient and ungovernable. Grotius maintained that there is an international society in operation composed of sovereign states.

This work does not presume that any of them has right perception of international society than others. It takes note that the three competing patterns (traditions of thought) had been co-existing through out time 'dynamically interweaving, but always distinct', in mutual tension and conflict. It further notes that all three patterns are simultaneously present in international thought and practice. Hence no one formulation is able to account from an empirical point of view, for the totality of international relations. But the three of them reflect the totality of international relations. Therefore a detail discussion is appropriate to relate the views of Gandhi, Nehru and Lohia with them.

HOBBESIAN CONCEPTION : THE REALIST DIMENSION

The Nature and Functioning of the International Society: Organizing and Operational Principles

Thomas Hobbes provides the principal impetus of what may loosely be called the realist position which interprets the world politics as essentially struggle of states for power in international relations. The tradition of power politics[1] (reason of states) dates back to the philosophy of Thomas Hobbes. His tradition is reflected in the writings of E.H. Carr, Reinhold Neibuhr, Hans Morgenthau, Herbert Butterfield, Bacon, Spinoza, Pufendorf and others.

Hobbes provides a systematic account of the rigorous logic of relations among independent powers that find themselves in a situation of anarchy in the sense of absence of government. Hobbes's account of anarchy tells us, with ruthless candor, not only how and why these powers do and must confront one another under the imperatives of international anarchy, but also what they should and sometimes can do to provide a modicum of security even while they remain in this condition.

The starting point of Hobbes's account of relations among states is the proposition that these relations are shaped in state of nature which is basically a war instinct. In such a state of nature, the states, like individual men find themselves in such a condition of war, if they are not in awe of a common power that is Leviathan. While referring to the state of nature, Hobbes describes the life of an individual before the contract came into existence, "but though there had never been anytime, wherein particular men were in a condition of war one against another; yet in all times, kings and persons of sovereign authority, because of their independence, are in continual jealousies, and in the state and posture of gladiators; having their weapons pointing, their eyes fixed on one another; that is, their forts, garrisons and guns upon the frontiers' of their kingdoms; and continual spies upon their neighbours; which is a posture of war."[2]

However, what Hobbes says about the life of an individual in the state of nature may be read as a description of the condition of states in relation to one another. According to Hobbes, the sovereign states in the international anarchy are in a condition of war and can not achieve peace in the absence of a common power to keep them in awe.

The Formation of State System

The Realists advocate a strong paradigm that the 'nation-state' do not compose international society as such. The nation-state system is an anarchical system as there is no common authority yet either by contract or by consensus to impose law and order upon them.

Sovereign states do not recognize any higher authority than themselves in the system. They, therefore, live in a state of nature. The "people" who live in the state of nature solve their problems of insecurity by instituting a sovereign Leviathan by means of a social contract. But the "states" thus created by contract have not yet created a 'global Leviathan', hence they live in a state of nature. Hobbes explains why people living in the state of nature create a sovereign authority (state) and create a domestic society (civil society) and that he does not care however, to advocate the creation of a global society by a social contract among the states.

Sovereign states, thus emerged by international social contract, simply (confine) locked themselves into international system, and do not constitute what we call an international society. Each state, thus, is encompassed in, what is called, the hide of a Leviathan and internally each Leviathan is politically independent of others. Under the garb of

Leviathan, each state in its external environment maintains its independence and right to exist and assert. For the realist school of thought, the formation of sovereign states does not terminate the state of nature *per se.* It simply transcends it to a higher plane of commonwealth that is at the level of international relations. Thus, a social contract creates a civil society of several sovereign states and puts an end to the problematic of insecurity. But the same contract may create international anarchy and the problematic of "state security" at the international level. Hence, the problematic of international insecurity remains unattended and unresolved for sovereign states.

The sovereign states do not recognize any higher authority than themselves and find themselves in perpetual state of nature. The international state of nature gives birth to the classic security dilemma and force them to live in a condition of mutual competition and conflict.

The Hobbesian tradition, thus, regards states as essential actors or units of analysis in international relations. In short, Hobbesian image of the world is a system of sovereign states, characterized by international anarchy, i.e., the absence of the centralized authority. Realism, therefore, denies the existence of an effective international society. For them international relations is a pre-contractual state of nature and no meaningful society can be contemplated out of it. In other words, what preceded the formation of state that is the state of nature was brought to an end through social contract resulting in 'civil society'. However, the state of nature which is characterized by confrontation, conflict and competition still continues for all sovereign states and that is the reality which constitutes the main theme of international relations, that is insecurity and anarchy — and therefore search for order.

Principle of Self-Help

According to Hobbesian conception, in an international state of nature, there exists separate 'states' among whom there prevails no natural tendency to live in a society. Every state is endowed with an equal natural right to self-preservation. It includes the right to do what is necessary to preserve the life i.e., the survival of state. The state is the sole arbiter of what, in fact, is necessary to expand one's liberty. For Hobbes, states are, with respect to each other, in a condition analogous to that prevails among individuals in a state of nature.[3] Each state has the same right in protecting the safety of its own body. The Realists school considers the state as a self-sufficient, non-moral entity. The sovereign authority and the unity of government are the essence of the state. Hence, in international relations, each sovereign state submits to no higher law than the safety of its own realm. Each state has an equal right to look after itself.

The Hobbesian school does not subscribe to the assumption that some common values, rules, interests and institutions bind states together in a society. The dominant characteristic of a nation-state system is "conflict" and not consensus. Actually, 'consensus' can be the basis of any society. There must be a 'unity of purpose' and 'unity of action' in a consensual society. While the state system can be characterized as a system of competing alliances which are occasionally interrupted by bloody wars. Hobbes is the first theorist who describes the relations among states explicitly in terms of the anarchic state of nature.[4]

On War

According to Hobbes the causes of war are three: (a) competition for material possessions, which leads to wars fought for gain; (b) diffidence or mistrust, the source of wars fought for defense or security; and (c) glory, the pursuit of which leads to wars to prevent others from undervaluing us and also from ignoring our opinions on faith. Hobbes's doctrine of the three great motives of war - gain, fear, and glory is reinterpretation of the doctrine of war propounded by Thucydides, a great philosopher historian of the ancient Greece. According to him, states generally resort to war mainly for three reasons, "chiefly for fear, next for honour, and lastly for profit".[5]

Hobbes views 'fear' in the sense of the rational apprehension of future insecurity, as the prime motive that affects, not some states at some time, but all states at all times. It is a concern to secure what we already have, rather than to aspire for what we do not have. This inclines all human beings toward "a perpetual and restless desire of power after power, that ceaseth only in death".[6] It is the motive of fear, leading to search for security through superior power. It works more significantly than competition for material goods or clashes of ideology, to put states into conflict with one another. For neither or none of contending states seeking security in this way can be superior.

Hobbes's argument rather points to the conclusion that the dangers can not be averted. The incompatibility of interests between two or more states, each of which is seeking security through superior power, does not rest on mistaken perceptions but is quite genuine.[7]

States are in a condition of war, not in the sense that they are always fighting but in the sense that over a period of time, they have a known disposition to fight. War in this sense is inherent in the condition of states that are not in awe of a common power; and peace, in a sense of a time in which there is no disposition to fight, is beyond their reach. There is a war of every state against every other state. At any point in time there might be relations of alliance or indifference between particular states as well as those of hostility. But over a long stretch of time every state will display its deposition to fight every other. There are no "security communities", or groups of states that have overcome the disposition to fight with one another.[8]

Amoral Society

According to the realist school, international politics is essentially amoral. Its proponents argue that such concepts as morality, justice, equality, law do not exist in international relations. The highest morality of a nation-state is self-preservation and *reason-d'etat*—the national interest. This means that the statesman's obligations are basically to his state, its government and its citizens and that the highest duty of all is to preserve and enhance national power. This school does not see any duty towards the mankind. Thus, the sovereign states are the amoral actors of international relations.

The question of morality refers to the expression of "good" and "bad". Nothing is "good" or "bad" for a state. It is a subjective matter for a state. In fact, "good" and "bad" refer to some objects of desire, and reveals only the pleasure and aversions of the human subject. Besides, there is no consensus on "common good" among sovereign states. Hence, the problem of the so-called international morality does not arise in the Hobbesian conception of international society.

Morality refers to a common conduct of states. But in international relations, one's own safety and happiness are the ultimate measures of conduct.

International Law

In the state of nature, according to Hobbes, there is no positive law, "no property, no dominion, no mine and thine instinct; but only that to be every man's, that he can get, and for so long as he can keep it".[9] For Hobbes, law is a command of the sovereign and can come into being only as a consequence of the establishment of the government. Princes and commonwealth, being subject to no common government, can not be subject to law. What is called the law of nations, in Hobbes' view, is not law or international law, in quite the same sense in which municipal law is. The law of nations, Hobbes maintains, is the same as the law of nature, that is to say, the prudential rules of survival.[10]

In the Hobbesian view, states are free to pursue their goals in relation to other states without moral or legal restriction of any kind. As the idea of morality and law are valid only in the context of a society, international politics is beyond society. If any moral or legal goals are to be pursued in international politics, these goals will be only of a state and not of a society. States conduct their foreign policy in a kind of moral or legal vacuum. The moral behaviour for the state in foreign policy lies in its own self-assertion. The states are neither guided nor are their behaviours restricted by any rules. If they are at all guided by any rules, they are the rules of prudence and expediency.

The Realist school later agrees that there is 'international law' but it is not, like the municipal law, meant to be observed compulsorily. International law is voluntary in nature. The states may or may not observe it. And only states can be the subject of international law and not the people who live within the sovereign states. In fact the so-called international law is only a set of 'rules and principles' and it may or may not be observed. There is no higher or competent authority to implement the international law.

It, therefore, logically follows that the "subjects" of international law can be independent states only. The international persons are only those collective persons on whom it is postulated that they have a moral nature analogous with that of individuals, making them capable of enjoying rights and assuming obligations. Thus, the international law recognizes only society of sovereign states and denies the existence of an effective international society.

The word "law" denotes a system of rules which is created and modified by a legislature, interpreted and applied by a judiciary, and enforced by the executive. These organs (legislature, executive and judiciary) are either non-existent or appear rudimentary in a nation-state system. hence the urgent need in a international relations is to establish a rule of law.

Even in this century, some states do not even take into account the existence of those international laws. For them, these laws are either defective or unjust or even if they observe them, they do so as a matter of expediency, not as a part of legal obligations.

The Concept of Justice

National interest is the sole guiding principle in Hobbesian society and in that light low premium has been attached to the principles of rationality, morality and justice. In order to pursue justice in international society, operationalization of perfect rational action is required. Perfect rational action requires perception of the tie between one's own state and other states and that all the states must be conscious of the nature of this tie. But, in international anarchy, no tie exist between states. Thus, justice is an irrational ideal. What is rational in this context is pursuance of national interest.

Moreover, relations among nation-states are not influenced by any consideration of justice. They are chiefly guided the 'power' consideration. The consideration of 'good will', 'general good', 'justice' do not influence the consciousness of the state nor do they provoke to shape action in the international arena. All states behave with excessive consideration of their "vital national interest" which shatters the edifice of social obligation and cooperation. Hence, the conflict is resolved by resorting to force. The entire system legitimizes the use of force in international system. To use force, or threat to use force are the sharp (ultimate, inevitable) ends of power politics in an anarchical society. Thus, recourse to violence is regarded as just.

The state is a solitary 'actor' in absence of a dependable order. It is always threatened by the fear of invasion of other states, in the neighbourhood. In the Hobbesian sense, the state is, thus, trapped into an inevitable competitive system for its survival. The dilemma it faces at this stage is whether to 'survive' or to seek 'justice' at the cost of its survival. Hence all of them succumb to the logic of power politics. In such a situation, the words like 'good will', 'amity', and 'friendship' acquire the status of rhetoric with least or no weightage. The utility attached to them is just to disguise the national interest of the state with a view to safeguarding and promoting it.

Whenever peace and order are disturbed in the international society, they are restored not by any consideration of justice, but by countervailing actions of states. At present the state-system is stratified in a hierarchy of 'great power', 'middle power' and 'small power'.[11] Whenever a state or a group of states are threatened by any form of hegemony, the states resort to the technique of alliances and counter alliances without any consideration of justice, good will etc. And thus, order (stability) is maintained in the system at the cost of justice.

Power Politics

The nation-state system functions in a legal vaccum; hence, the realist paradigm views international politics as a state of war by all against all. Hence, international politics is politics of power. It is a struggle for power in which each state is pitted against the other. International politics is nothing but pure conflict between states. For realists, politics is a zero-sum game. The interest of the state excludes interest of any other. That is why wars break out periodically between nations of the world. Peace may be understood as a period between two wars. It is infact a time to prepare for the next war.

The nation-state system, which operates in a state of nature, considers wars as natural phenomena as there is no order between states. The Commonwealth are enemies by nature. If one state wishes to attack another, it may do so. It can wage war by right. All that is necessary is to have a will to do so. Later Realists agree that states need not be in a permanent state of hostilities. Agreements to act in concert for the benefit of each may be entered into. But, they remain in force as long as the fear of loss or hope of gain remains among the beneficiaries. Each state as a party to the alliance has the right to breach the treaty whenever it wishes. It can not be accused of violation of any covenant. Thus, in a state of nature, each state may give a promise which is meant for breaking. Each one as an equal is subject to the universal urge to self-preservation.

According to Hobbes, by nature man is not rational, but selfish. He is subject to passions. His actions are determined by desires and passions. They are not constrained by inward moral sense. His supreme goal is to fulfill his desire irrespective of moral choice. On the international level, the 'states' behave like "individuals" with a psychology of the state of nature. Individual states having no common political superior exist in the same relation to each other as men that of in the state of nature.[12]

Spinoza assumes that the state of mutual conflict between individuals in the state of nature, which is resolved by the establishment of sovereign states, is then transferred to the relations between sovereign states. Pufendorf, another thinker in the line of Hobbes, is aware of bad conduct of the state, but which he blames not the state, but, the unorganized international society.[13] He believes that greed and lust for power motivate the behaviour of the state. In an international state of nature, there is "war", "preparation of war" or "unsettled peace". Pufendorf maintains that 'peace' without precautions does not guarantee security of the state. If peace is desired, Pufendorf counsels, the best way is to be prepared for war.[14] The evil oppression and treachery can shatter the fabric of human order.

The Hobbesian school upholds the doctrine of deterrence, and considers it just, legal and moral. The absence of a common superior enhances the dignity of each sovereign. If peace is broken, the affected state can use force against the aggressor to any degree, it thinks, desirable. It is a natural right of the state to defend itself. If the injury is slight, the sovereign may use whatever degree of violence necessary to ensure security against future aggression.[15]

Spinoza sees natural condition of man as that of an endless conflict. He also agrees that "to avoid war of all against all" it is necessary for an individual (in a state of nature) to vest sole power coercion in one individual or a group superior to him. Thus, the sovereign becomes powerful. Spinoza, thus, sees power, rather than some moral ideal, as the fundamental concept in the nation-state system.[16] Hence, it is natural and essential for the state to acquire more and more power.

The nation-state system of today is, in fact, born out of religious wars which went on for thirty years in Europe. The emerging society of independent sovereign states, sanctified by the treaty of Westphalia,[17] was to be governed by power relations. The constant tensions and conflicts were a part of the system. Thus, states which were born out of religious conflict, survive by conflict.[18] In this way the war is in built into the system. The institution of war is an inevitable part of the international life. Likewise, the phenomena of wars form an inevitable aspect of international relations.

Each state in the sovereign-state system believes that other states always try to destroy them and, therefore, they must also be always ready to destroy others, whenever the need be, in order to protect themselves. Even the modern realists such as George Kennan, Hans J. Morgenthau, Henry Kissinger etc., believe that international politics, like all politics, is a struggle for power. Thus, the basic assumption of the existence of conflict among nations remains the same among the classical and the neo-classical thinkers. Each nation seeks national interest which can be viewed only in terms of power.

The neo-realists maintain that the struggle for power is the hall-mark of today's politics and the game of power-politics is neither controlled, nor regulated by the international law or by the world government. In the absence of overarching global authority, the international anarchy is (mis)managed by the devices and doctrines of balance of power;

balance of terror; the collective security system; the alliance system; and by the (mis)use of international institutions by regime formations, nuclear deterrence, crisis management, detente, arms control and transfer of arms and technology etc.[19] Thus, the threat system preserves order in international society.

The realist or Machiavellian conception denies the existence of an effective international society, as they maintain that society can only be established by contract. Hence, for the realists, the current international relations is in a pre-contractual state of nature. The sovereign state system is just a provisional/tentative arrangement and no meaningful society can be contemplated out of it.

According to Hobbes, the 'domestic society' came into being by social contract, hence the domestic system connotes to the 'civil society'. The international system, being pre-contractual, refers to 'the state of nature'. The basic pursuance of the domestic society is to achieve good life. In international system, the basic problem is the survival of states. The government is the principal source of domestic order, but as the (world) government is absent in international society, it is an anarchical society. The sovereign state system is vulnerable, defective and fragile. Then, how can international order be maintained in the absence of a world government? For Hobbes, there is no order, there is chaos.

To sum up, for the Realists, the sovereign states do not compose international society as they operate on the principle of self-help. War is therefore natural in that society. The idea of justice as well as of morality does not have any place in that society. It does not have any agency to create or maintain order, hence the reality of naked power politics becomes the operational principle of international chaos.

KANTIAN CONCEPTION OF INTERNATIONAL SOCIETY : THE REVOLUTIONIST DIMENSION

The Nature and Functioning of International Society: The Organizing and Operational Principles

Kant, like Hobbes, in his famous pamphlet, 'Perpetual Peace' conceives the world as a system of sovereign states, characterized by international anarchy or having absence of centralized authority. Kant conceives that at the present stage of history international society is composed of independent states. They have their sovereignty. They are autonomous in relation to each another. However, they feel insecure against each other, as they are not bound by either a common authority or a common law. Hence they live in anarchy and are all the time in search of perpetual peace. Perpetual peace can't be established untill the real society composed of human beings is organised. For Kant, the existing community of states is 'unreal'—a complex of legal fictions and obsolescent diplomatic form which conceals, obstructs and oppresses the real society of individual men and women, the *civitas maxima*.[21] According to Kant, the community of mankind exists potentially, even if it does not exist actually. Kant believes that the dominant theme of international politics seems to be the relationship among states, but it should be the relationship among all men in the community of mankind. He further maintains that when the community of mankind comes into being, it puts the system of states in limbo. Thus, Kant identifies individuals, and not states, as the true members of the international society. However, Kant does not want to reject the present structure of the society of states, he considers it illegitimate and temporary in nature in the long run.

Kant agrees with Hobbes regarding the anarchical nature of international society. But he believes that the individual (decision-makers) within the state operate in international society on behalf of the state. Thus, the individuals manage the affairs of the state. The individuals are more important than the sovereign state *per se*. Hence, Kant presumes that behind the legal facade of the fictitious Society of Nations rests the true international society composed of men.[22]

The problem is how to create a 'society of men' out of the 'society of states?' For this, we need to escape international anarchy. But, before we enter into the discussion of how to escape international anarchy, let us discuss other features of Kantian conception of anarchy.

Insecurity

Like Hobbes, Kant depicts the bleak picture of the state of nature. It is full of chronic and unmitigated insecurity. Kant compares international insecurity with that of individual men living in a state of nature before the 'state' came into existence by social contract.

People who have grouped themselves into states may be judged in the same way as individual men living in the state of nature, independent of external law; for they are a standing offense to one another by the very fact that they are neighbours.[23]

Kant, however, does not relate insecurity to actual fighting between the states, or even to the frequency of war. He presumes that insecurity is fundamental characteristic of the state of nature, Kant writes, "But man (or an individual) in a mere state of nature robs me of any security and injures me by virtue of this very state in which he coexists with me".[24] He further writes, that there is a "lawlessness" in international society and it is a 'permanent threat to peace'.[25]

Kant in his book, '*Metaphysics of Morals*' describes international anarchy: "In their external relationship with one another, states, like lawless savages, exist in a condition devoid of right... this condition is one of war (the right of the stronger), even if there is no actual war or continuous active fighting".[26]

Like Hobbes, Kant also believes that international society is composed of sovereign states and the dominant theme of international society is anarchy. But Kant's perception of international anarchy is somewhat different from Hobbes. For him, international anarchy is managed by the existing international law and by the system of the balance of power. These are inadequate devices to create a perpetual peace on the globe. Now let us examine Kant's views on international law and, balance of power.

Anarchy and International Law

The sovereign state system, Kant believes, creates fractions in the mankind and also helps in keeping the fractions intact. The present form of state system does not have capacity to achieve permanent peace because, the institution of war is in-built into the system. War itself is corruptible in nature. It is a source of evil and moral corruption. The institutions of 'war' is built into the society of states and hence does not allow the establishment of "rule of law" between the states. As a result, men cannot enjoy freedom. The global society is organized by mankind which is regulated by a genuine international law.

Kant, like Hobbes, believes that international law can be conditionally valid only until the state of nature is abandoned. He further believes that the existing international law is inadequate and on that ground no progress towards peace can be achieved. The existing international law does not have slightest legal force, since states as such are not subject to a common external constraint.[27]

In the final phase, Kant believes that the achievement of a more satisfactory 'law governed external relationship' is a long-term goal that can only be reached gradually and with much difficulty. He maintains that in the meantime, the existing international law draws its force from common interest and reciprocity. He advocates for abiding by them until a true international law emerges out of the agreements between all sovereign states.[28]

Phenomenon of War

For Kant, war is a complicated phenomenon. It can't be prevented at one stroke. In order to prevent war, we have to understand its complexity.

According to Kant, war breaks out between nations as a result of three factors operating at three levels. at one level, it is the product of human nature. Kant shares with Hobbes a pessimistic view of human nature. He speaks of depravity of human nature and 'man's selfish and criminal instinct'.[29] Kant interprets that war does not seem to require any kind of motivation for it is very much ingrained in human nature.[30] At the second level, frequency of war is clearly influenced by the character of domestic governments. He blames despots who have war like inclination. The ruler has a glory to maintain. In order to be more and more glorified, he wills to 'order thousands of people to immolate themselves for a cause which does not truly concern them.'[31] At the third level, he argues, war is a fundamental and intrinsic characteristic of international anarchy that exists between states. He refers here to the security dilemma that nation-states face while dealing with each other.

Kant is convinced that in order to solve the problem of war, we must come to terms with each of these three sets of problems. Indeed, the real significance of a republican government is that it provides a link to relate these three levels. According to Kant, the republican form of government restrains human nature and helps in reforming the domestic society. He further assumes that the reformed domestic society will ultimately bring improvement to the international anarchy. By the term 'republic', Kant means a constitutional state with a separation of powers.[32]

Like Hobbes, Kant believes that the social contract creates a domestic society (civil society), but simultaneously the same contract also creates international anarchy. The international "state of war" comes into existence with the disappearance of "internal state of war". He, however, disagrees that social life is possible without first tackling international state of war (international anarchy). This anarchy seems to be managed: (i) by the existing international law, and (ii) by the device of the balance of power. If they are inadequate principles they need to be perfected. Nevertheless they help in surviving the nation-state system and help men to survive even after being totally slaughtered in case of a sweeping war. Kant relates the existing international law and the device of balance of power to the condition of war.

Kant maintains that the state of nature permits states to wage war. He states, "In the state of nature, the right to make war (i.e. to enter into hostilities) is the permitted means by which one state prosecutes its rights against another. Thus, if a state believes that it has been injured by another state,it is entitled to use violence, for it cannot in the state of nature gain satisfaction through legal proceedings".[33]

In the absence of 'legal proceedings', Kant maintains, the existing international law and the balance of power "restrain" the conduct of war. Thus, the law helps in restraining the states who wage war. The existing international law derives its effect and strength from sovereign states as it is in their mutual interest to obey it. What is it in the 'mutual interest' which forces states to obey the law?

It is in the mutual interest because the existing law will not, "allow".. "the attached state" to use "any means of defense" that would "render its subjects unfit to be citizens". Besides, the existing international law also takes care of that, "No state at war with another shall permit such acts of hostility as would make mutual confidence impossible during a future time of peace".[34]

He further writes in "Perpetual Peace" that it helps in preventing "dishonourable stratagems" during and after the war. He specifies to such acts as "the employment of assassins" or 'poisoners', breach of 'agreements', the instigation of treason within "the enemy state, and the like". The existing international law prevents 'war' to turn into a war of extermination'.

Balance of Power

According to Kant, so long as a 'civil society' is not established at the international level, it is necessary to 'regulate' hostility prevailing between sovereign states. And this hostility can be regulated by law of equilibrium i.e. balance of power.

Kant justifies even the instinct to wage war in the interest of maintaining balance of power. Speaking of "alarming increase in the power of another state", Kant argues, "this is an injury to the less powerful state by the mere fact that the other state, even without offering any active offence, is more powerful.. On this is based the right to maintain a balance of power among all states which have active contact with one another".[35]

In another work, "The idea for a Universal History", Kant seems to accept the necessity for a law of equilibrium, while referring the idea of equality of sovereign states within an anarchical society. He writes about "a principle of equality governing the actions and counter actions of these energies, lest they should destroy one another", although he never believes that the principles of international law and balance of power can ever bring perpetual peace. To emphasize his point he explains: For a permanent universal peace by means of a so-called European balance of power is a pure illusion, like Swift's story of the house which the builder has constructed in such a perfect harmony with all the laws of equilibrium and yet it collapses as soon as a sparrow alights it.[36]

Thus, Kant understands the utility of international law and the balance of power as fragile operating principles of the functioning of international anarchy.

Transforming Strategy

For Kant, neither existing international law, nor the balance of power provides an adequate answer to the problem of war. He is very clear in arguing that peace must be formally established: "Peace can neither be inaugurated nor secured without a general agreement between nations".[37] What kind of general agreement does he suggest? The most logical way to end a lawless state of nature, would be to form an international state through a universal union of states (Volkerstaat) (in allgemeiner statenuerein). "There is only one rational way in which states can emerge from a lawless condition of pure warfare. Just like individual men, they must renounce their savage and lawless freedom, adopt themselves to public coercive laws and, thus, form an international state (*civitas gentium*) which would necessarily continue to grow until it embraces all the peoples of the earth".[38]

Thus, Kant suggests to establish the universal union of states as a part of his transforming strategy in order to have perpetual peace.

Confederation of Place of Universal Leviathan for Moral Improvement

Before examining the transforming strategy of Kant for a "world republic" (pacific union) for transforming the nation-state system, it is necessary to understand why he does not suggest creation of an international Leviathan or a single world government or (international state) at one stroke?

In his view a civil society cannot be created overnight by a single contract as the society of states (nation-state system) is too rigid to give away immediately. Secondly, "states" are the "units" of the international society, and not the individuals, (as they were in the state of nature). They are different from individuals. They are so much used to their internal liberty, equality, rights and sovereignty, that they will not be ready to "subject" themselves to a "wider constitution" (Leviathan). In the third place, Kant argues that states are totally different in terms of languages used and religion followed by their peoples. These factors separate them and prevent them from intermingling. The fourth and the most powerful argument against the idea of an international state is that it is both impractical and contrary to the idea of freedom. He writes in "Perpetual Peace": "For the laws progressively lose their impact as the government increases its range and a soulless despotism, after crushing the last germs of goodness, will finally lapse into anarchy".[39] While emphasizing the same idea in his another work, "Metaphysics of Morals", he writes: "But if such an international state of this kind extends over too wide an area of land, it will eventually become impossible to govern and hence to protect each of its members and the multitude of corporations this would require must again lead to a state of war".[40]

Kant, in his book in "*Theory and Practice*" (1793), first rejects the idea of cosmopolitan commonwealth under a single head (in weltburger-liches gemeines Wesen unter cinem oborhaupt) because of the danger of such a state leading to "the most fearful despotism".[41] This idea of Kant is graphically highlighted in, "*The Philosophy of Kant*" edited by Carl Friedrich, "Each separate state, so long as it has a neighbouring state which it does hope to conquer, strives to aggrandize itself through such a conquest, and thus to attain a world empire, a polity wherein all freedom and, as a consequence, virtue, taste, and learning, would necessarily expire. Yet this monster in which laws gradually lose their force, after it has swallowed all its neighbours, finally dissolves of itself, and through rebellion and disunion breaks into many smaller states. These, instead of striving toward a league of nations, a republic of federated free nations, begin the same game again, each for itself, so that war, the scourge of humanity, may not be allowed to cease".[42]

Thus, Kant views war as not so incurable an evil as the resulting universal autocracy (out of straight forward international social contract). Kant, in this way, does not see any viability or desirability for an international state (Leviathan). Instead he advocates the creation of a federation of separate states.[43] He favours a 'lawful condition of federation, with a commonly agreed international law (in rechtlicher zustand der Foderation nach einem gemeinschoftlich verabredeten Volkerrecht).

As argued above, Kant is against creating a social contract amongst sovereign states at once because he is convinced that this type of social contract can not create a "social life". He firmly believes that social life is not possibly created at international level until the problem of war is tackled.

The problematique of war can not be solved by legal contract between states. The contract creates only union of states, and not a civil union of mankind. The civil union of mankind from within the states gradually leads to a civil society of mankind. Republican states create an awareness of universal civil values among the people which furthers the creation of a civil society.

A Scheme to Abolish War

Kant does not want to abolish the state system at a stroke. But he wants to improve it. He wants to subject international anarchy to law and to find a solution to the problem of war. But, he wants it in such a way that the essential autonomy and independence of states may not be sacrificed. Thus, Kant's primary concern is with order at the level of inter-state relations. He does not see the solution to the problem of war in terms of a merger of states: "It was no more logical to hope to solve the international problem by the super session of the states than it would have been to try to end the civil strife by the abolition of individuals".[44] By federation of states, Kant means only a loose league of republican states, that have come together for the sole purpose of abolishing war.

Broadly, Kant suggests three dimensional strategies to create a civil society of mankind out of the society of states. These three dimensions are not separate or hierarchical in character. They must function simultaneously at the same time. These strategic dimensions are :

1. The creation of a loose-federation out of the existing nation-state system. In other words, the rearrangement of existing units within the existing international anarchical system in such a way to help to create a civil society amongst the people of the states;
2. Moral improvement of domestic system; and
3. The moral improvement of individuals.

Kant advocates a federation of free peoples, a kind of league, which might be called a pacific federation.[45] This federation does not aim to acquire any power like that of the state, but merely to preserve and secure the freedom of each state in itself along with that of all the other confederated states, although this does not mean that they need to submit to public laws and to a coercive power which enforces them as men do in the state of nature.[46]

Thus, Kant advocates law governed external relationship, but never under the tutelage of a single power. Kant, as a gradualist, hopes that his ideal federation will not come into existence overnight, but gradually, each nation will realize its necessity and will come forward to form it. One day it will become a truly universal federation. he also knows well that if such a federation is not able to become truly universal, its effect would be merely to rearrange the units within the international anarchy, rather than to overcome that anarchy. Such a federation appears to Kant as the limit of what is possible, given the constraints of state sovereignty and the importance of state autonomy on one hand, and the need for a lawful framework for international relations on the other.

This federation creates conditions for the existence of international right to exist and prosper. There can be no public right without this type of federation. And any right which can be conceived outside the federation is considered within the state of nature and these rights are then termed as private rights, and not public rights.

On advocating this type of federation, Kant is aware of its weaknesses and its limitations on playing its role on international scene. He knows that whatever he is advocating is not revolutionary. It is just to make the federating units (states) more effective by rearranging them within international anarchy. Kant thinks that such a limited federation will serve two purposes:[47]

1. that it will shift one's attitude to war by reinforcing normative constraints on the use of force in international relations;

2. that it may not abolish the institution of war, but at least it will regulate and curb underlying causes of war.

Hence, for Kant the civil union of states is one step ahead in the direction of creation of a civil society. The global civil society can not be created until the loose federation of separate states is created from above and a perfect civil union of mankind from below. Thus, Kant advocates, not legal contract between states outright, but civil union for a creation of global civil society.

The Main Characteristics of Federation

Kant outrightly rejects a positive idea of a world republic in favour of negative substitute in the shape of an enduring and gradually expanding federation likely to prevent war. He wants a federation of free peoples, a kind of league, or a 'pacific federation'.

Kant does not want that states should give up their sovereignty altogether. He advocates, in fact, total independence of states and wants to uphold a strict principle of non-intervention. He never wants that any other state or any outside authority should interfere in internal affairs of the states. He desires only law-governed external relations; among states and not the 'amalgamation of the separate nations under a single power'.

Under any circumstances, Kant does not want any type of internal intervention within the federating units. In fact, the principle of non-intervention provides inter-state order. Non-intervention will not only preserve the inter-state order, but also strengthen the tie between states. Kant thus rejects very emphatically both the desirability and the validity of any move towards world government. On the contrary, Kant wants states to be economically, politically and military powerful and self-reliant. According to him, only self-sufficiency will provide for genuine cooperation among states. Kant, while referring to a loose federation, writes, "the benefit of federation could be enjoyed without the costs of continuous struggle and instability' and where stability rests both on the internal strength and cohesiveness of states and on the universal acceptance of each other's indépendence and legitimacy".[48]

Kant further sees that this type of federation will strengthen international legal order, as it consolidates the existing mutual rights and duties among states.

Kant is not only against, external intervention within the state, but also against giving the right to rebelion to the citizens of the state. He fears that right to rebellion will kill the spirit of republican form of government and, ultimately, will affect the structure of the pacific federation. As such international federation has to be a great bulwork against the danger of international anarchy.

Finally, Kant is strongly against abolishing the state as an entity. According to him, it give, its citizens linguistic, historical and cultural identity. Moreover, it organizes people socially and thus provides a social framework for individual freedom.

Moral Improvement of Domestic System

In order to establish perpetual peace, Kant emphasizes the process of domestic reform. Some aspects of this reform is related to a domestic form of government. Kant advocates a civil constitution and a republican form of government for internal functioning of the state. By the term 'republic', he means a constitutional state with a separation of executive and legislative organs of the government. Thus, eventually, he advocates a democratic form of government for establishing perpetual peace. He is convinced that a republican form of government preferably stands for peace. He also presumes that the 'people' are more naturally inclined to peace more than their bellicose rulers. Peace is more likely in a republic because the power to restrain the aggressive tendencies of rulers lies in the hands of the people. He says: "...each state must be organized internally in such a way that the head of the state... must no longer have the deciding vote on whether war is to be declared or not, for the people who pay for it must decide..."[49] He, presumes that people know that war causes misery, injury and risk of death to them. This further deters people to declare war against adversary. Kant does not believe that people are always peaceful or virtuous. He does believe that progress towards perpetual peace ultimately depends upon moral upliftment of individuals. Yet such progress in turn, can only come about within a good political constitution as it renders positive climate to such efforts. Kant advocates a republican form of government as it provides a framework within which moral progress is possible.

The second aspect of domestic reform is related to the military of the state. Kant favours militia against professional armies.[50] He pleads to disband the existing armies as they are expensive, and politically oppressive and encourage arms race. In a republican form of government, people experience consequences of war directly. Moreover, he thinks that the state will have to keep armies so long as international anarchy remains, and so long army remains, anarchy continues. But Kant gives a solution to this dilemma. He is convinced that abolition or, atleast, reduction of domestic army will lead to minimization of international anarchy and, thus, will ultimately be a step ahead in the direction of achieving perpetual peace.

Moral Improvement of Individual

In social science, there is a tension between two paradigms: 'Individual' and 'society'. The dilemma is: which of the two should be privileged for human progress and social justice? Kant does not suffer from this dilemma. He suggests improvement in the both simultaneously.

Kant's scheme of domestic reform has been discussed. Now it is equally essential to discuss his (moral) philosophy as regards improvement in individual. His philosophy is solely based on the assumption that human beings are capable of discovering and acting upon moral imperatives which are universally valid/acceptable.

At present, the most powerful of these moral imperative is to find a means to abolish war. While exemplifying, Kant writes, "Now, moral-practical reason within us pronounces the following irresistible veto: There shall be no war.... Thus, it is no longer a question of whether perpetual peace is really possible or not.... we must simply act as if it could come about, and turn our efforts towards establishing that constitution which seems most suitable for this purpose".[51]

Kant firmly believes that forceful and repeated statements on immorality of war serves an essential purpose in helping to shape the normative climate in international relations. Kant argues that what is necessary is to change the attitude of people towards the use of force in settling differences between two states. The changed attitude of the people will affect the behaviour of a state. Thus, Kant insist on evolving a value system for a possible global society.

Secondly, Kant believes that the individual has a moral capacity to learn from experience and to act on that acquired experience. One's ability to learn from experience is a central feature of Kant's moral view. Out of experience the mankind has realized that unless international anarchy is reformed, increasingly destructive conflict will be inevitable. According to Kant, man possesses a great moral capacity and is 'animated by respect for right and duty'.[52]

The third kind of moral improvement concerns gradual process by which an individual becomes increasingly capable to see himself as a part of a global community. Man, in future, may not have such realization from the political point of view. He will see himself as a part of interdependent economic spheres, that is the phenomenal growth of global trade and commerce. This development will not result into a man denouncing his obligation to the state. But the range of moral obligations he needs to announce will expand beyond his nation. He will feel morally interdependent; such cultures will be enhanced by the need of the time and, as a result, all men will come closer. This will further lead 'toward a general agreement on the principle for peace and understanding'.

Yet, Kant can never be satisfied simply with moral improvement of individuals and of domestic society. It is only when international anarchy is reformed through a formal agreement between states that progress towards perpetual peace is possible. Therefore, progress towards perpetual peace is based on moral improvement and self-interest, and on a combination of factors working at levels of individual, domestic society and the international system.

Kant and Perpetual Peace

According to Kant, perpetual peace can't be established immediately by establishing a world government by any form of contract or agreement. The world government can be created only by abolishing the present state system. He is not interested in abolishing the society of states, but he constantly wants improvement and perfection in it. In the beginning, Kant's aim is to achieve, in the words of Barry Buzan, 'mature anarchy'.[53]

In mature anarchy, the benefits of fragmentation can be enjoyed by the state without the costs of continuous struggle and instability. Stability rests on the internal strength and cohesiveness of states and also on the universal acceptance of each others' independence and legitimacy.

Kant is in favour of strengthening the international legal order by his scheme of limited pacific federation in such a way that it can protect the autonomy and independence of states. He wants to treat the existing international law, however inadequate it may be, as a building block for his great edifice of perpetual peace.

The components of internal order of the state-constitutional state with a republican form of government; moral and political rights of citizens; and the principle of intervention- are not subversive to inter-state order, but complementary to means of perfecting its functioning.

Kant suggests some structural reforms to the existing system. But ultimately, it is still a 'state system'. Kant does not mind if his limited pacific federation ultimately becomes a working system of peace in which, there will be a central government to enforce the law and to limit or curb the sovereignty of the states. He does not mind this type of structural reform if it leads to perpetual peace. But cosmopolitanism need not mean that he wants to abolish nations or national frontiers. He wants that "nations" must embody man's (not only states) moral, and to a certain degree, his political rights and duties.

Thus, Kant is primarily concerned with individuals and does view the inter-state system as having a derivative significance on them. The impulse for progress towards perpetual peace comes largely from the individual; from the outrange at the destructiveness of war, from the ability to learn from experience, and from the gradual moral improvement of mankind. The starting point of Kant's moral and political philosophy is individual, his moral freedom. From that base, he is then led to consider the kind of domestic society and international society.

Like any other serious thinker, Kant experiences a great tension while facing a choice between "statism" and 'cosmopolitanism'. On one hand, the existing state system has not outgrown its utility and it is deep rooted. On the other, there is a considerable amount of moral pressure and practical demand for the creation of a cosmopolitan authority. But his way of facing the tension is novel and unique. His compromising formula is equally unique. He maintains that 'what is moral within a domestic society, can also be moral between the states as states are composed of men and states further compose after all, a civil society.

Moreover, Kant believes that the choice is not between 'total anarchy; and total (legal system) civil society. The change and progress should not be viewed as a choice between the continuation of the state of war (Hobbes) and the complete transcendençe of the state system and its replacement by some form of universal political organization. The change and progress lies in reforming the existing sovereign state system.

Kant, however, does not provide a single solution to the problem of war. Although he accepts the reality of international anarchy but it is unacceptable to him. It becomes Unbearable as the destructiveness of war increases. But he does not want to put an end to anarchy by creating an international leviathan and by abolishing a state system, because it may degenerate into a condition of universal oppression. Theoretically, optimal solution of creating an 'international super state' would involve a loss of the state's positive functions as a provider of localized order and protector of linguistic and patriotic loyalties. Any ideal solution need be based on a rationale of balance between the reality of state sovereignty and the need to provide a firmer basis for those institutions and obligations that work to curb excesses of that sovereignty.

His moderate scheme of a limited pacific federation is a short term device to improve upon the functioning of a nation-state system, which hopefully, ultimately might lead to a long term solution. His scheme of pacific federation is a half way compromise between the positive functions of state system and the practical difficulties of trying to reform it.

Kant is convinced that the pacific federation, which will create a transnational ties of many type, will generate powerful ties of mutual interest, that would provide an important impulse towards perpetual peace.

To conclude, Kant, like Hobbes, views the present international society of states as anarchical but he differs regarding the nature of anarchy with Hobbes. For Kant, the phenomena of war is the main cause of anarchy as it breeds insecurity and prevents the rule of law to prevail. Moreover, war breaks out now and then between the states, as there is no civil union of mankind. In order to create a civil union of mankind, Kant suggests three-prong strategy: (a) moral improvement of men; (b) moral improvement of domestic society; and (c) a creation of a confederation of sovereign states. Kant was convinced that if these type of measures are taken, the real society of mankind can be created out of the fictitious society of sovereign states. If it happens, the perpetual peace can be established. The international law and the device of the balance of power try to create order but they are inadequate hence war breaks out in a society of states.

GROTIAN CONCEPTION OF INTERNATIONAL SOCIETY: THE RATIONALIST TRADITION

Nature and Functioning of Society: Organizing and Operational Principles

Grotius views the international society as composed of sovereign states. The states and their rulers in their dealings with others are bound by rules and together formed a society. On one hand, princes and peoples have indeed become independent of each another and, as a result, people are relieved from the central authorities (according to Westphalia treaty, all the states and people became free from the Roman Empire). They are the sovereigns in the state. However, on the other hand, Grotius maintains that they are not in a state of nature, but a part of a wider society of all mankind (*magma communities humani generis*). Even without central institutions, rulers and peoples may constitute a society among themselves, an anarchical society or a society without government.[54]

Grotius, thus, rejects the formulations of Machiavelli, Hobbes or Bacon that sovereign states and princes in their dealings with each are in a state of nature, unrestrained by bonds of law or society. In the absence of societal or lawful restraints, the states are free to conduct policies towards one another according to the dictates of the new idea of reason of state.[55] Grotius also differs from the conception evolved by Kant that the present form of international society characterized by sovereign state is fictitious and transitory in nature. The states and princes can be made subject to a central authority. By this, they can escape from the state of nature into which they appeared to be drifting. Grotius views that international politics is taking place within an international society in which states are bound not only by rules of prudence or expediency, but also by imperatives of morality and law.[56] Grotius further explains that the threat that holds the international society together is a 'core of common standards and common customs which is embodied in international law. The society of states can be called international society because all the sovereign states are bound by international law. The states, and through them, individuals living in them are bound by international law. Thus, states and individuals are operating themselves within the boundaries of international law.

Grotius identifies 'states' as well as 'individuals' as true members of the international society. In the absence of a common global authority, sovereign states will exercise its authority over individuals. Grotius accepts that a sovereign state is a primary actor in the international society, but he also accords a particular status to individual under international law.[57] This is attributable to his theory of essential identity of an individual and the state which in turn reflects a 'patrimonial conception of the state and the influence of natural law theory. Grotius maintains that along with states individuals also hold rights and owe duties under international law. Further, as states are composed of individual human beings they as well as the state are subject to rights and duties under 'international law'. Further, as states are composed of individual human beings they as well as the states are subject to rights and duties under 'international law'. The recognition of the rights of individuals under the law of nations is made possible by the assumption that natural law, and not positive law, or voluntary law provides the ultimate source of moral and legal obligations.[58]

Thus, according to Grotius, states are composed of individual human beings and, by that credit, an individual becomes the basic unit of law. Grotius rejects the doctrine of the 'reason of state' and denies that individuals and states are subject to different standards of morality.On the basis of the identity of an individual and the state, he posits that both are subject to the same moral and ethical standards and restraints.[60]

Grotius on Reason of States

Grotius considers man as moral, social and rational. Therefore, he gives 'man' the centrality of law and rejects any dominant place for 'reason of state'[61] in inter-state relations. He presumes that states wielding great power can afford to pursue their policies without any regards to law and solely in the light of their own advantage. Secondly, no state is so powerful that it can afford to dispense with the help of others. Such is the impact of economic inter-dependence and of military security.

The Grotian tradition takes into account existence of states which exercise valid political authority. Thus, it recognizes the moral claim of the state to be there and to be counted. The claim of the state as a political authority may be accepted relatively, and not absolutely. Secondly, they do not consider society of states as a sole arbiter of human destiny, but as a part of the greater whole. This school of thought does not see international society as ready or keen to supersede domestic society. It notes that international society actually exercises restraints upon its members.

Grotius on War

Grotius begins his contemplation with the assumption that war is inevitable and, indeed, 'is in perfect accord with first principles of nature, for the aim of war is the preservation of life and limb'.[62] He, however, denies the Hobbesean conception of world in terms of a system of sovereign states, characterized by international anarchy, or the absence of centralized authority. He also rejects the conception of international politics as a 'state of war' in which the absence of effective centralized restraints results in a "war of all against all". By evolving a doctrine of natural law, Grotius provides the normative framework for the newly emerging states system.

The corner stone of the Grotian conception of international society, is 'natural law' which provides a normative framework for the state system. The natural law forms the basis of international society. The 'states' and 'individual' are subject to international law. The same international law permits war for "life and limb". The Grotian theory permits war for the preservation of life and limb and he calls it a 'just war'. He distinguishes between just and unjust wars and permits just wars within international society.[63] But the theoretical basis of the just war, for Grotius, is the law of nature. Grotius defines the law of nature: as "a dictate of right reason".[64]

Grotius asserts that the law of nature is the law that is in the most conformity with the social nature of man and the preservation of human society. The law of nature in its primary sense prohibits the taking of what belongs to others, demands restoration to others of what is their property, imposes duty to fulfil promises and to make reparation for injury, and confers the right to inflict punishment.[65] In other words, it fulfills the requirements for 'just war'.

Grotius is convinced of the reality of a society of states just as there is a society of men comprising a state. In default of judicial proceedings, war is the method adopted by states to settle their claims.

From these premises, Grotius advances his key proposition that a war initiated without a basis in strict justice is an 'unjust war'. The just causes of war are based on natural law and the law of nations. They extend to:

1. defence against an injury, actual or threatening, but not anticipatory;
2. a recovery of what is legally due to the aggrieved state; and
3. the infliction of punishment upon the wrong doing of states.[66] By this scheme of thought, Grotius accepts the reality of war as a phenomenon recognized by the law, but at the same time seeks to eliminate unlicensed and unrestrained resort to war by demanding 'just' and legal grounds for wars.

Grotius is clear about the just cause. He does not allow war to be waged on the grounds of potential threat to the security of a state. As he believes that human life exists under such conditions that complete security is never guaranteed to us.[67] Thus, wars waged without any 'cause' are 'unjust'. A treaty of alliance is not binding in relation to a state waging an unjust war. Moreover, he is very clear about the duty of a citizen during the war. Grotius is firm that a subject ordered to take up arms in an 'unjust war' has the duty to refuse.[68] On the question of 'neutrality' during the time of war, Grotius propounds a novel doctrine of 'qualified neutrality'. In fact, international law can, in theory, establish that some wars 'unjust' and criminal and yet demand that neutral states act with absolute impartiality as between the aggressor and the victim state. Such a posture would be, in legal terms be open to doubts and, in moral terms, manifestly wrong. In order to solve this dilemma, grotius writes: It is the duty of those who keep out of war to do nothing whereby he who supports a wicked cause may be rendered more powerful, or whereby the movements of him who wages a just war may be hampered..[69] This does not imply a duty to assist actively those waging the just war, nor does it debar the right to do so. Grotius asserts that the right of passage ought to be denied to a state waging an unjust war, while it ought to be granted to a state waging a just war.[70]

Reason of state is contrary to Grotius 'main theory concerning the 'just war', 'namely', that there can be no right to resort to war unless there is a just and legal cause for it.

Grotius thinks that the law of Nations has as its purpose the advantage of all the members of the great society of states and not that of one particular state.

Throughout his writings, Grotius makes his reader aware of his dislike of war although he does accept war as a legal institution. He believes that it is not possible to achieve some legal regulation of the conduct of warfare if war itself is not recognied by law.

Grotius' conception of 'just war' is derived from his primary contention that the totality of international relations are subject to the rule of law, including the resort to war and the conduct of warfare.

In his formulation of the distinction between 'just' and 'unjust' war Grotius rejects the doctrine of 'reason of state'.[71] His idea of qualified neutrality of states flows from his doctrine of 'just war'.

Grotius' great moral principles are : (i) resort to war and the conduct of warfare should be subjected to law: and (ii) recourse to war should be based on justice and not 'reason:

1. Grotius defines the problematique in terms of the phenomena of war and conditions of peace and order. He is less concerned with the causes of war than with the conditions of peace and order, reflecting the belief that war is inevitable.
2. Grotius, thus, does not believe that international society is a fiction or illegitimate. he rejects the idea that states will wither away or the society of states is transitory in nature.

Grotius is essentially conservative, as he does not advocate the replacement of the existing order with a new order. He is basically concerned with creating a normative and legal framework for the emerging states system by which the relations of sovereign states may be subjected to the rule of law. Hence, he does not suggest any transforming strategy.

Neo-Grotian School of Thought

Martin White and Hedley Bull are chief among the neo-Grotians. They have essentially reinterpreted the Grotian doctrine on international relations. The Regime theorists, viz., Krasner, Oran Young, Donald

Puchala and Taymond Hopkins are also called neo-Grotians. Although they define the problematique in terms of the phenomena of war, peace and order, the gist of their arguments is incorporated in this section in order to understand the modern interpretation of Hugo Grotius.

Neo-Grotians : Martin Wight : Bull and Regime Theorists
Martin Wight

Martin Wight frames the problematic in terms of war and identifies states as the chief participators in international politics. The image of the world advanced is that of anarchy. He maintains that "mutual mistrust is fundamental" in international relations.[72]

— Wight is less concerned with the causes of war. He is interested more in conditions of peace and order. War for him is inevitable.

— Wight rejects the view that the only subjects of international law are the states. He wants to encompass the role of individual and non-state actors.

— Wight believes that a 'core of common standards and common customs' which is embodied in international law does not bind the 'states' alone, but also 'institutions of international society' (and non-state actors).

— Wight, like Grotius, reflects the image of a world as a society of sovereign states as anarchical in a sense that it lacks a central authority. But it is orderly due to the regulating influence of the rules, institutions and practices of international society.

— Wight however agrees that international law is rooted in common standards and practices of international society. But it lasts for a long time, and survives mainly because of the positive institutions and practices of international society — diplomacy, balance of power, and other functional international institutions.[73]

— Both believe in the legitimacy of present order and thus, give 'states' a primary importance. But both of them, unlike Hobbes, make the states subject to the moral and legal restrains embodied in international society. Thus, Grotius and neo-grotians differ from the classical formulation of Hobbes of international society as an anarchical society.

Wight accords membership in international society to both the states as well as individuals. Thus, he is very near to the natural law tradition. The ultimate source of obligation to Wight comprise consent and custom emerging out of constitutionalism and rationalism. Thus, Wight's international society is constrained by the constitution of a state constitutionalism, which limits the exercise of power by the states.

Hedley Bull as a Neo-Grotian

— Bull, like Grotius and Wight defines the problematique in terms of the phenomenon of war and the conditions of peace and order. But he is more concerned with the problem of 'order'. He does not offer sustained analysis of the causes of war but prefers to explain the existence of 'order' in anarchy.

— Bull is a classical thinker and firmly believes, unlike Grotius, that the states are the essential actors in international relations and hence primary units of analysis.[74]

Bull is against granting legal personality to individuals. However, he advocates that mankind should be organized as a society of sovereign states.[75] He also grants that the other non-state actors (transnational actors) have not so successfully challenged the primacy of states. Why should he grant their claim to be equal with state and thus legitimize them to carry 'the seeds of subversion of the society of sovereign states'?[76]

Bull rejects the Grotian notion that natural law forms the basis of international society and the foundation for individual rights and responsibilities. He like positivists, claims that the common norms, values and customs are created by states and not by abstract theories about what states should do.[77] The right and duties are created by states and not by international law.

Bull accepts the society of states as a primary thing, but rejects the claim that international relations is a pre-contractual state of nature devoid of any social elements. He also does not agree that a 'universal empire' or a 'world state' is going to replace states system in near future.

Bull maintains that there is no agreement or consensus regarding the criteria which should govern the state action. States are capable of agreeing only for some minimum purpose and not for the enforcement of law. He further argues that there is no universal consensus as to right and wrong conduct in international relations.[78] Bull rejects the Grotian distinction between just and unjust wars on the grounds that international society is often divided as to which side embodies the just cause.

Bull recognizes the existence of international society like Grotius (unlike Hobbes) but, it is not based upon universal natural principles of right and wrong conduct. Bull's international society consists of the positive rules, practices, and institutions of international society which embody common interests and values of states.[79]

There are international laws, but there are "areas of actual (mutual) agreement between states'. For Bull, there are no rules that are valid independently of human will, that are part of 'nature'.

Bull identifies international law, the balance of power, great power management and war as common institutions of international society. The mutual respect for the territorial integrity and independence of states, belief in the sanctity of promises, and in certain limitations, on the use of force constitute common interests of its members. These common interests in turn reflect the value that state attaches to the goals of preserving the society of independent and sovereign states. For Bull, the society of states is the fundamental reality of world politics today.

Regime Theorists as Neo-Grotians

Krasner identifies Oran Young, Donald Puchala and Raymond Hopkins as neo-Grotians. They are known as Regime theorists, because they interpret the problematique in much the same terms as does the Grotian tradition. At the most fundamental level, they define the problematique in terms of the conditions of order in international relations. They discuss and study the phenomena of regime creation and transformation. But they are ultimately concerned with accounting for cooperative and rule governed behaviour in an anarchical system.[81]

The idea that a less than a universal a more limited society may exist in pockets or in areas of actual agreement amongst states is reflected in the works of international regimes analysts. Students of international regimes are generally concerned with the issues of governance and, hence, focus upon the formal and informal rules, institutions and practices that regulate international relations. Regimes have been broadly defined as governing arrangements constructed by states to coordinate their expectations and organizing aspects of international behaviour in various issue-areas.[82]

The important thing to note is that the common norms and values which are said to characterize regime governed activities originate not in natural law principles, but in the positive actions of states. Thus, regime theory is not a natural-law-theory of society or community but an interest-based theory which traces the cooperative elements of international relations to more realist concerns of utility, expediency and power.

Finally, the regime theorists are called neo-grotians mainly because their theory lacks the natural law origins. It seeks affinity with the classical tradition; it emphasis positivism. It gives concession to power politics as it reflects positive regimes and biased regimes.[83] Their notions of society, regimes and areas of co-operative state relations challenge the classical assumption that a system of sovereign states is necessarily disorderly and incapable of producing co-operative patterns of behaviour of any more than a rudimentary character. There are formal and informal, explicit and implicit rules, and institutions and practices regulating the behaviour of states, despite the structure of anarchy. Bull attempts to combine the notion of society with the realist assumptions of the classical tradition. he also augments the classical tradition by showing that anarchy is not synonymous with disorder and by turning attention towards areas of informal, co-operative and norm-governed behaviour in international relations.

Grotius and neo-Grotians presume that the sovereign states form an international Society. They, however, differ regarding the nature of order in that society. Grotius believes that international law provides order in society. While the neo-grotians believe that order is maintained by custom, convention and other international institutions, viz. Alliance System, Balance of Power, War, the Collective Security System etc. Thus, for the Grotians the international society is orderly in nature and it should be maintained. They do not see any need to change, improve or transform the existing society composed of nation-states.

The subsequent chapters on Gandhi, Nehru and Lohia will relate their views with those of Hobbes, Grotius and Kant not in a comparative fashion, but categorically. The next chapter tries to ascertain views of Gandhi on the nature and functioning of international society. What type of order that society prescribes and whether Gandhi is satisfied with it. If not, then what strategy does one need in Gandhi's conceptions?

NOTES AND REFERENCES

Notes on Hobbes : Realism

1. The term "power politics", (The reason of states) has been defined differently by the different scholars. Thomas Hobbes grants right to every state to ensure its own survival and that links him to the tradition of reason of states. he advocates the ultimate freedom of states from moral fetters so far as the objective of self preservation is concerned. He allows any state to take any measure necessary to achieve this objectives (but Hobbes excludes the use of mere brute force on the

pursuit of power for its own sake). The word brute force on the pursuit of power for its own sake). The word 'power politics' is a translation of the German world Machtpolitik, which means the politics of force —the conduct of international relations by force or the threat of force, without consideration of right or justice. About the time of the First World War, the concept of power politics developed by the Realist superseded an older and more elegant phase, raison d'etat, which implied that statesmen cannot be bound in public affairs by the morality they would respect in private life, that there is a `reason of state' justifying unscrupulous action in defense of the public interest.

It means that there is a reason of state justifying unscrupulous action in defense of the public interest, the term power politics focus upon a central truth about international relations. According to Martin Wight it suggests the relationship between independent powers and we take such a state of affairs for granted. It implies two conditions. First, there are independent political units acknowledging no political superior, and claiming to be 'sovereign'; and secondly, there are continuous and organized relations between them. This is the modern system of state. We must note in the conclusion that common usage, power politics means, not only the relations between independent powers, but something more sinister. Schwarzenberger believes that power politics signifies a type of relation between states in which certain pattern of behaviour are preponderant: Armaments, isolationism, power diplomacy, hegemony, imperialism, alliances, balance of power, balance of terror and war. He emphasizes these characteristic of international politics. He maintains that under the system of power politics, "each group considers itself not as a means of a common end, but as an end in itself".

Thomas Hobbes lived from 1588 to 1679. *Elemental Philosophical Deceive* was published in 1642 and republished in 1647. Leviathan was published in 1651. For a summary of Hobbes' influence upon international theory see, e. Dickinson, "*The Equality of States in International Law*", Chapter III, (1920).

2. Thomas Hobbes, "*Leviathan*", in the English works of Thokmas Hobbes of Malmesbury, edited by Sir William Molesworth, 11 vols.; J. Bohn, London1836-45, Vol. 3, p. 115. Anarchy; the concept of Anarchy describes as social state of affairs in which the power of the state has either been removed or crippled in the exercise of its official authority. A state of lawlessness or absence of government is called

anarchic. In international relations this phrase made famous by Goldsworthy Lowes dickinson. He for the first time used the concept of `International anarchy' in the sense of the absence of government or rule among sovereign states, unlike the individuals within the states, are not subject to common government. See the European Anarchy, Allen and Unwin, London, 1926. Professor Hedley Bull conceptualized it by publishing his famous book: "*The Anarchical Society : A Study of order in World Politics*" Macmillan, London, 1977. Hedley Bull, Hobbes and the International Anarchy, republished in Preston King (edt.) Critical Assessments of Leading Political Philosophers: Thuomas Hobbes: Critical Assessments, Vol. III, published by Routledge, London, New York, 1993. P. 81. The article was originally published in: Social Research, Vol. XLVIII, No. 4, Winter 1981, pp. 717-38.

3. Coted in H. Bull. Op.cit., p. 81.
4. Cornelius F. Murphy, Jr., "The Grotian vision of world order". *The American Journal of International Law*, Vol. 76, p. 484.
5. For detain description refer I,; Arend Lijphart, "The Structure of the Theoretical Revolution in International Rclations", *International Studies Quarterly*, Vol. 18, No. 1, March, 1974, p. 44.
6. B. Bull, Ibid., p. 82.
7. Cited in, H. Bull, Op.cit., p. 82.
8. Ibid., p. 82.
9. Ibid., p. 81,82.
10. Cited in H. Bull, Ibid., pp. 82-83.
11. Ibid., p. 82.
12. Ian Clark, "*The Hierarchy of States : Reform and Resistance in the International Order*', Cambridge University Press, Cambridge, 1989, pp. 1-9.
13. Cited in Cornelius, Op.cit., p. 488.
14. Cited in Ibid., p. 489.
15. Cited in Ibid., p. 490.
16. Ibid., p. 490.
17. Ibid., p. 485.
18. The treaty of Westphalia was concluded among by European states in 1648 after the thirty years religious war among them. By this treaty the thirty years war was concluded and the sovereignty of all the princes (both Catholic and Protestant) was recognized within their respective domains. All the states were declared free from all jurisdiction of the Pope or any Catholic authority. Along with this,

the Holy Roman emperor's was bound not to interfere with the administration of the independent states. In fact the emperor was stripped of all important public and translational authority. The text of the westphalia recently published in F.L. Israel, (edt)., "*Major Peace Treaties of Modern History*", 1967. As the authority of the Holy Roman Emperor rapidly declined, a `system of states' emerged in world politics.

19. Lijphart, p. 489.
20. H. Bull, "*Anarchical Society*", pp. 101-200.
    Notes on Immanuel Kant (Revolutionism)
21. Martin Wight, "Western Values in International Relations"., in Butterfield and Wight, (edt.), "*Diplomatic Investigation*", London, 1966, p. 93.
22. Martin Wight, "The Anatomy of International Thought", in *Review of International Studies*, 13,3 July 1987, pp. 223-224.
23. H.B. Nisbet, "Perpetual Peace", in Hans Raiss, (edt.), "*Kant's Political Writings*", Cambridge, 1970, p. 102. Perpetual Peace (Suhr Kamp Verla) was first published in German in 1985.
24. Perpetual Peace, Reiss, p. 98.
25. Ibid.
26. The Metaphysics of Morals, p. 165.
27. perpetual Peace, Reiss, p. 103.
28. Ibid., p. 107.
29. Perpetual Peace, Reiss, p. 103.
30. Reiss, Idea for a Universal History with a Cosmopolitan Purpose, p. 42.
31. Perpetual Peace, Reiss, pp. 95 & 103.
32. Ibid., p. 104.
33. Reiss, The Metaphysics of Morals, p. 167.
34. Perpetual Peace, Reiss, p. 9. Also see M.G. Firsyth Sopar, "*The Theory of International Relations : From Gentil to Treitsehke*", Allen and Unwin, 1970, p. 204.
35. Reiss, The Metaphysics of Morals, p. 167.
36. Ibid., p. 92.
37. Perpetual Peace, Reiss, p. 104.
38. Ibid., p. 107.
39. Ibid., p. 113.
40. Reiss, The Metaphysics of Morals, p. 171.
41. Kant on the common saying: 'This may be True in Theory but it does not Apply in Practice, in Reiss, p. 90.

42. Carl Friedrich, (edt.) "*The Philosophy of Kant*", New York, 1949, p. 381.
43. Reiss, p. 47.
44. Hinnsley F.H, "*Power and the Pursuit of Peace*", Cambridge, 1980, p. 62.
45. Perpetual Peace, Reiss, pp. 102 & 104.
46. Ibid., p. 104. Kant's 'perpetual peace' has been interpreted differently by the different thinkers. But the main schools of thoughts are prominent: One is called 'Statist' paradigm of Kant's writings and the other is called 'Cosmopolitan' or Universalist school of thought. The Statists argue that Kant is primarily concerned with order at the level of interstate relations. He did not want to transcend the state system but to improve it. He wanted to subject the international anarchy to law and to find a solution to the problem of war but in a way which would not sacrifice the essential autonomy and independence of the states. This view makes a case of Kant's rejection of world government. Kant was not against the idea of the world government but he was the great advocate of the autonomy of states and his insistence on the importance of non-intervention. Kant believed that the progress depend not on any plan for the reform of the state system but on the internal improvement of states and in particular, the achievement of republican government. This tradition underlines the limited nature of Kant's view of cosmopolitan law and in Kant's view, federation of states means only a "loose league of republican states that have come together foe the sole purpose of abolishing war. This view is strongly advocated by F.H. Hinaley, in "*Power and the Pursuit of Peace*", first published in 1961. Hinsley stresses that Kant did not see the solution to the problem of war in terms of a merger of states.

    The other school of thought was originated with the idea of Martin Wight and this idea was subsequently developed by Hedley Bull. According to Bull Kant does hold out a universal republic as an ideal in which the international anarchy would be resolved by the creation of a *Civitas Gentium*. bull reluctantly comes to accept the negative substitute of a pacific federation. The advocates of cosmopolitan aspects of Kant put forward these arguments in justification: (1) For Kant, the interstate system is only passing phase and international life should be viewed in terms o f a global society of mankind; (2) the conflicts results either out of enlightenment or by the promoting of a vested interest; (3) Kant's advocate international morality and imperatives to move towards a more peaceful world. This work agrees with the views of Bull on plea that Kant never wanted merely to rearrange unit (states) within the Anarchy. He was in search of a solution of Anarchy.

47. Andrew Hurrell, "Kant and the Kantian Paradigm in International Relations", in *Review of International Studies*, Great Britain 1990, 16, p. 194.
48. Bary Buzan, "*People, State and Fear*", London, 1983, pp. 96-97.
49. Reisss, pp. 90-91.
50. For further reading refer to, Theory and Practice, Reiss, p. 90.
51. The Metaphysics of Morals, in Reiss, p. 174.
52. Theory and Practice, Reiss, p. 92.
53. Barry Buzan, "*People, State and Fear*", Second edition, Boulder, Co., Lynne Rienner, 1991, pp. 96-97. Also see on `Mature Anarchy', Ken Booth, "Security in Anarchy: Utopian Realism in Theory and Practice" in *International Affairs*, Vol. 67., No.3., July 1991, p. 530.

Notes on Hugo Grotius (Rationalist Tradition)

54. Hedley Bull, "The importance of Grotius in the Study of International Relations", in Hedley Bull, Benedict Kingsbury and Adam Roberts, (edt.) "*Hugo Grotius and International Relations*", Clarendon Press, Oxford, 1992, p. 72.
55. Ibid., p. 72.
56. Hedley Bull, "*The Anarchical Society: A Study of Order in World Politics*", Macmillan, London, 1977, pp. 24,26, & 27. Bull also says: `The Grotian or solodarist doctrine seeks to achieve a more orderly would be restricting or abolishing resort to war by individual states for political ends, and promoting the idea that force can legitimately be used only to promote the purposes of the international community.
57. Claire Cutler, "The Grotian Tradition in International Relations", in *Review of International Studies*, Vol. 16, Great Britain, 1990, p. 45.
58. Ibid., p. 45.
59. Grotius identifies three categories of law: natural, divine and voluntary or positive law comprises both municipal law and the law of nations, both of which derive form the consent of their subject.s However, Grotius roots the obligatory nature of consent in natural law and thus gives positive law a naturalistic base. See Grotius, War and Peace, Prolegomena I, p. 16; Briefly, Basis of Obligation, p. 10, and Lauterpacht, Grotian Tradition, pp. 21-22.
60. Grotius perceptions of self-interest are infused with concerns for the common goods. Grotius refuses to concede that every animal is

impelled by nature to seek only its own good and argues that the law of nations has in view the advantage, not of particular states but the great society of states. (For details, see Prolegomena, pp. 11-15) JBW/Prolegomena refers to the Hugo Grotius works translated in English known as Kelsey translation, classics of international Law, edition, 1925.

61. Cornelius F. Murphy, Jr., "The Grotian Vision of World Order", *The American Journal of International Law*, Vol. 76, 1982, p. 483.
62. Grotius, War and Peace, Book I, Chp. 2, p. 52, For further reference see Prolegomena 8; Book I, Chapt. 2. and Book II and III.
63. By justifying 'War' on the ground of just causes Grotius sought to strike a middle ground between the two contending views on the legitimacy of warfare then prevalent in Europe. On the one extreme, the Pacifists believed that the use of arms could not be reconciled with a Christians conscience. on the other extreme, who maintained that all wars commenced by sovereign will were lawful and the practices of warfare were not subject to moral restraint. Moreover, Gtotius was convinced that the justice will not be silenced by the clash of arms. The redress of wrong was a principle of natural law, Grotius being a jurist by professor, he legalized the recourse to arms by the state provided it begins for the just cause. But the war must be fought within the boundaries of a national law. For Grotius if the war undertaken by lawful authority and for proper reasons, warfare constitutes an enforcement of law and right. If conducted according to moral precepts, Grotius' reflected that it will lead to peace as it ultimate goal.
64. According to Grotian tradition, the essential distinction between man and other animals is the faculty of reason. It means power to discern the good rather than the faculty of logical thought. The action of the lower animal are determined by desire and passion. They are not constrained by and inward moral sense. Man's dignity lies in a voluntary conformity to rule.
65. Grotius, War and Peace, Book I, Chp. 2. o. 52.
66. G.I.A.D. Draper, "Grotius: Place in the Development of Legal Ideas about war" in H. Bull, Benedict and Adams, (edt.), "*Hugo Grotius and International Relations*" Glarendom Press, Oxford, 1992, pp. 192-201.
67. Ibid.
68. Ibid.
69. Grotius, War and Peace, Book I & II.

70. Ibid.
71. Draper, p. 202. As Grotius denies that individuals and states are subject to different standards of morality.
72. Martin Wight, "Power politics", Edited by Hedley Bull and Carsten Holbraad, Licester University Press, 1978, pp. 101-102.
73. Martin Wight, "Western Values in International Relations", in Butterfield and Wight, "*Diplomatic Investigations*", p. 93.
74. Bull, Anarchical Society, p. 24.
75. Ibid., p. 152.
76. Ibid., p. 153.
77. Ibid., p. 35.
78. H. Bull, "The Grotian conception of International Society", in H. Butterfield and M. Wight, (edt.), "*Diplomatic Investigation*", Cambridge, Mass, 1968, p. 52.
79. Bull, Anarchical Society, p. 43.
80. Ibid., p. 67 & 70.
81. "International Regimes: Towards a New Theory of Institutions" in *World Politics*, 39, 1986, p. 111.
82. F. Kratochwil and J.g. Ruggie, "International Organization: A State of the Art on the Art of the State", in *International Organization*, 40, 1986. p. 759. For a useful review of the regimes literature, see Haggard and B.S.Simmons, "Theories of International Regimes", in *International Organization*, 41, 1987, pp. 491-517.
83. Puchala and R.F. Hopkins, "International Regimes: lessons from Inductive Analysis", in Krashner, (edt.), *International Regimes*, pp. 61-90, p. 66. and Haggard and Simmons, "Theories of International Regimes", p. 493. criticizes the formulation of Regime theorist for overstating the normative consensus in international politics by assuming that all regularities in behaviour are rule governed, thus 'conflicting' such 'patterns' with 'rules'.

Chapter 2

GANDHI'S CONCEPTION OF INTERNATIONAL SOCIETY

This chapter examines Gandhi's conceptions of international society and analyses the type of (dis)order it creates. It also conceptualizes Gandhi's strategy for improving as well as for transcending the existing unjust international order.

Nature and Functioning of International Society

Intuitively, Gandhi presumes, like Kant, that there is an international society and it is composed of mainly two elements: (1) nation-states; and (2) Mankind i.e., individuals at base.[1] Now we will discuss his views on both these components, one by one.

Gandhi and Nation-State

To Gandhi, nation-state appears as two odd phenomena, the 'nation' and the 'state', subsumed under one single entity. The concept of nation represents, according to him, a meaningful combination of individuals, each with a distinct potentiality of his own to fulfil a common mission. The state, on the other hand, is a mechanical arrangement super-imposed on a nation. For Gandhi, nation stands for creativity and vitality, while the state is an archetype of convention and conservatism. Gandhi, therefore, wants to make sure that social potentiality of nation-hood should not be eclipsed by an overwhelming concern of the state to ensure conformity of the people to its political and military prescriptions. Gandhi never wants the state to stifle the creativity of the people as a so-called controller of the destiny of a nation.[2]

Whenever Gandhi writes on 'state', he painfully points out imperfections and dangers of modern state. He seeks to cut it (state) to its size by propounding a social theory in which the state largely loses its deceptive luster and turns into a mere necessary evil. While expressing his fear upon increasing the power of the state, Gandhi writes, "I look upon an increase in the power of the state with the greatest fear because although while apparently doing good by minimizing exploitation, it does the greatest harm to mankind by destroying individuality which lies at the root of all progress."[3] The state does not possess moral personality or entity as it is an artificially devised mechanism which is bound to be value-neutral. Human intervention whether 'moral' or 'immoral' shapes it into what it becomes. The entire history of political thought deals with the question of 'how to transcend from the notion of 'is' to 'ought'; but, for the human concern for good life, 'ought' would have never been an agenda for reformers. The state, being a legal structure, can hardly obtain just order with the help of law alone. Unless the state, as a legal instinct, transcends its limitation, it can not be come ideal to achieve the denied goals of peace, order and justice.

For Gandhi, the operationalizing principles of International Society are mainly two: the 'force' within the state (violence), and the feeling of nationalism among the people. He considers these two — the feeling of nationalism and the force of arms and army — the basis of nation-state system. In other words, nation-state projects itself in international society by the ideology of 'nationalism' and by the display of army and modern weapons. Nation state, in another sense of the term, is an attempt to strike compatibility between its identity which rests on its rooted and cultivated characteristics and its legal structure.

Armaments and Army

The 'state' (which is an organized violence) projects its 'force' aspect in international relations through its accumulated sophisticated arms, weapon system and by well organized and well-trained professional army. The army which is not only loyal to the state, but also having patriotic feeling for a nation, and which is keen to sacrifice themselves and eliminate other in a total war. Every state thinks that it will become powerful if it builds armaments. It upgrades its security vis-a-vis other states.

Gandhi outrightly rejects the thesis that states get their strength by armaments. If the nation-states needs armaments, Gandhi believes, it means that the international order is ill-organised, and that something is seriously wrong with the system. It is fallacious to believe that the standing army gives nations the 'deterrent' power as well as a sense of security. The deterrence emerges from the conviction in the enemy that the entire nation will fight tooth and nail. According to Gandhi, strength does not come from armaments.

The real strength, Gandhi believes firmly, comes from self-sacrifice, from within the not through physical force. He advises nations to strengthen themselves spiritually. Real safety comes from innocence. He writes, "...it is really forgotten that safety which an individual derives from innocence is safety which no amount of arms will give you."[4]

The idea of 'peace through war' is ridiculed by Gandhi. From him it is a misconception and hypocrasy. Peace can never be achieved by the disastrous means of war. Gandhi has no faith in the idea that nuclear deterrence (balance of terror) will prevent war. Gandhi maintains that at best the destructive capability of these weapons may temporarily postpone the outbreak of war.[5]

Gandhi views the root cause of armament lust, on the part of the nation-states, to dominate others. If there is no greed, there will be no need for armaments. States arm themselves mainly because, they are afraid of each other. Generally, 'force' is used when people are under the spell of fear and what is gained through fear is retained only as long as fear is present.[6] Exploitation and fear give birth to phenomena of war, and nuclear weapons are the natural consequences of it. There is no hope for peace in the world, Gandhi believes, so long as the lust for dominance through power and exploitation, is not curbed.

Disarmament : Abolition of the Means of Violence

Gandhi suggests immediate solution of arms race. He advocates total disarmament. He denounces the idea of arms control. For him, armaments are both a symptom of force and a temptation to use it. By total disarmament, he means to remove, not only symptom of force but its temptation as well. Gandhi stands for total, complete and universal disarmament.

Mental Disarmament

In the context of mental disarmament, Radhakrishna is worth quoting: "War begins in the minds of men where it could be prevented". Gandhi pleads that the states should, first of all, disarm themselves mentally. People must reject armaments psychologically. Nations must disarm themselves with inner-most mental conviction that arms race is disastrous and will ruin the entire international society. Gandhi wants people to create public opinion and environment against armaments. He believes that if people are convinced from within, they will influence the decision making power of the state. He firmly believes that the elite can play vital role in this. For Gandhi, inward mental disarmament will lead to the total world disarmament. And the total world disarmament will be the only visible sign of that inward mental disarmament. Peace can be secured only by total disarmament.[7] Gandhi advocates that first mental disarmament should be achieved. This means that, he is against enforcing it on nation-state. He knows that no state can be taught discipline by compulsion, it is to be learnt by its own will.

Gandhi is realist enough to understand that the idea of total disarmament can never be operationalized overnight. It is time consuming to convince people and create favourable opinion by which people would determine to seek some arrangement alternative to the ideal of 'security through armament'. The alternative to armaments suggested by Gandhi is 'non-violence' (non-violent army). Gandhi firmly believes that people will have to learn to fight by non-violent means which will eventually be the weapons of all nations. Although Gandhi is optimistic, he knows the human nature. He knows that man learns slowly and only after paying a price for it.[8]

The real disarmament can only be effected provided the nations of the world cease to exploit one another. For Gandhi, nations build armies not to deter other nations or to invade, the chief purpose of a modern nation is to exploit other nations economically. In order to hide this motive, nation justifies its building of armaments in the name of security.

Unilateral Disarmament

Gandhi advocates a policy of unilateral disarmament before general or total disarmament is achieved. He appealed to the Great Powers of his time to take initiative in disarming themselves. He expressed, "Peace will never come until the great power courageously decide to disarm themselves".[9] He had great faith in individual initiative. All good things, Gandhi believed, begin with one single person. He urged that initiative towards disarmament should be taken soon by some country. He pleaded to Great Britain to take initiative in this direction and set the example. Gandhi wrote, "Some nation will dare disarm herself and to take large risks. The level of non-violence in that nation... will be unerring, her decision will be firm, her capacity for heroic self-sacrifice will be great and she wants to live as much for other nations as for herself".[10]

In unilateral disarmament, Gandhi views a bold but perfectly feasible course of action. Unilateral disarmament, however, will not eradicate international anarchy at one stroke but, according to him, it will be a new step in that direction.

Nation and the Power Hungry Elite

Gandhi views the nation-state as two odd phenomena, but according to him, the nation-state system operates mainly because of violence on the part of state and of the feeling of oneness amongst the citizens of a nation. Gandhi recognize 'nationalism' as an organizing principle of the people at the national level, but the same principle functions as disorganizing or dysfunctional principle at the international level. At domestic societal level, nationalism unites people of different colour, castes, creed and culture. Nationalism is directly connected with the feeling of patriotism. Patriotism makes us to forget our differences or helps us tolerate those differences. Thus, feeling of nationalism unites people within the states. Gandhi wonders how it can divide nations at a global societal level. It is astonishing for him, Gandhi asks, how nationalism a binding element within a nation becomes a fragmenting force at international level?

Gandhi argues how can 'nationalism' teach us to hate other nation when the same feeling of nationalism teaches us to love our fellow citizen at the national level. Hence, for Gandhi 'nationalism' *per se* is not bad but blandness lies with those who hold power in a state. The selfishness and the spirit of exploitation nurtured by the power wielder at the national level impel them to fight with others and prosper at the cost of others. Greedy rulers exploit positive feeling of nationalism and teach people to ruin others. Hatred for other nation is not an independent attribute of nationalism.[11] According to Gandhi, the principle of nationalism itself should not be blamed for its dyfunctionality at the international level. The real blame lies with the selfish leaders of the nation-state who exploit this principle to make it dysfunctional or disorganizing one.

Negative Nationalism

Gandhi does not condemn feeling of nationalism *per se*, but if, in its name national leaders preach hatred for other nation it has undesirable repercussions at the international level. People are made to think in terms of 'myself' and 'others'. The elite in the nation do so, especially in the West, because it helps them to stick to powers in their nations. The lust for power and greed in national leaders create hurdles in the way of removing international anarchy. To Gandhi, one's love for one's own nation is not desirable "such a love is an armed peace".[12] The main problem for Gandhi is how to persuade and change national leaders who preach and practice narrow and selfish nationalism.

While he blames the West for spreading feeling of negative nationalism Gandhi describes it as too much materialistic, selfish and narrowly nationalistic. What one requires is an international mind, which would ponder over welfare and spiritual advancement of all mankind.[13]

Positive Nationalism

Gandhi, therefore, pleads for positive nationalism, which is another form of internationalism. It teaches nations to learn to live for each other. In Gandhi's thinking, nationalism which teaches hatred for an -other nation is not in tune with positive nationalism. Nationalism can become reality only when people of different countries and cultures are organized in such a way that they are capable of acting as one entity.

But we can not develop internationalism because leaders of nations persuade people that if the feeling of nationalism is extended to the society of states, they may loose their identity as a nation. To Gandhi it is a misplaced fear. Nationalism is not against internationalism. Gandhi believes that internationalism pre-supposes nationalism, and not a narrow, selfish, greedy spirit that is often spread under the name of nationalism.[14]

Gandhi's Conception of Nationalism

In Gandhian conceptions of nationalism, lies the under-current of co-operation and understanding of one people by others in the spirit of humanity and sympathy, rather than in that of arrogance. Gandhi's positive nationalism, is, thus, a part of internationalism. His nationalism does not mean to have any malice, ill-will or contempt for others. It means to have only "good will and peace". He proclaims, "my nationalism is intense internationalism". His patriotism includes good will for mankind in general.[15] The ultimate goal of humanity, to Gandhi, is to achieve brotherhood of all people in the world. It can be achieved provided we convert (the principle of) negative nationalism into a positive one which teaches us to unite, and never to divide. In Gandhi's views, nation-state system can further be strengthened by the ideology of nationalism. The sovereign state-system is weak until the rise of the feeling of nationalism. By that, if becomes the nation-state system. The feeling of nationalism on the part of a citizen makes the system rigid. The national leaders exploit the feeling of nationalism for their narrow selfish motives. The rise of narrow nationalism within the nation makes the system even more anarchical. The two world wars were the horrifying results of the nation-state system prevailing in the first half of the twentieth century. In spite of the horrifying and bitter experiences, people of the world passed through the system have not improved. The peoples have still remained victims, of narrow nationalism. Gandhi, therefore, wants nationalism to become a force compatible with internationalism.

The main problem for Gandhi is not, therefore, 'nationalism' as such, but how to persuade national leaders not to preach and practice (narrow negative and selfish) nationalism. Gandhi does not see any tension between 'nationalism' and 'internationalism' because they operate at two different levels.He also does not see any contradiction between these two powerful forces. Gandhi is convinced that internationalism is a mere extension of nationalism and the unifying factor is the people, and not the state, irrespective of their diverse identities. In this sense Gandhi integrates nationalism with internationalism and wants it to be 'human centric' in nature.

Gandhi's Notion of Natural Law

Like Grotius, Gandhi intuitively evolves a notion of Natural Law. However, there is a difference between them. Grotius propounds a theory of natural law which is basically binding to the mankind as a whole. Gandhi derives has notion from the Indian notion of Dharma.[16] The Indian notion of Dharma is interpreted as an all pervading principle of Harmony and of mutual interdependence among all elements of nature and society. It is the principle of 'Truth' which, according to Gandhi, prevails ultimately. It is called 'Natural' because it re-asserts itself when disturbed. It is the same everywhere and at all times. It is 'Sanatana, i.e., Eternal. The Gandhian social theory is simple because SAT as 'Atman' pervades in each member of a society, and society is a system (Rta) in which sub-system (members) are interdependent entities.

As against the Western tradition of an intellectually postulated natural Law, Gandhi emphasizes an intuitive factor, common to the whole humanity, which he calls 'SAT' at the impersonal level and 'Atman' at the personal level.[17] By virtue of this common factor, human society is a system whose members are governed by the law of interdependence. These members can be nations, regions or individuals. the unity of the whole, which expresses itself through the cordial relations of the parts and filial relations among individual persons, is the basic law. Humanity, therefore, has to be organized to secure an unimpeded operation of this law against elements in the world which would like to harm the interests of mankind or its part.[18]

The fundamental Law

According to Gandhi, man and institutions formed by him function within the gamut of the fundamental law of universe. Gandhi's fundamental law refers to the fundamental unity in the universe which sustains order and life. Hence man, normally does not live by destruction. While referring to it, Nirmal Bose interprets that, Gandhi has drawn that law from history which operates behind universal processes.[19] Many may call it as beyond one's knowledge; although it is there all the same. Under the influence of that law, mankind makes progress, in course of time, towards a deeper realization of the essential unity of life. Barriers between communities can be pulled down gradually with the help of this law.

The chief purpose of human life is realization of the fundamental law of universe. Then it is the duty of every individual to set his life in accordance with the law. He has to help in the historical process of social progress. If we wish, then, to break down narrowness which cramps the growth of human life, which is either inherited from the past or handed down by institutions founded in the past, our method of change should also be informed by a higher degree of brotherhood among men. While trying to non-cooperate with institutions, we should bear no ill-will for our opponents, but should seek patiently to convert them through self-suffering. Finally, opponents have to be turned into willing partners with us in creating a new order of life based upon a sense of human unity.

The law of manual labour, according to Gandhi, is a moral law of life. All men have to share the common toil for preservation of life. Such a toil will deepen the feeling of fellowship among men.

A civilization based on equality is possible only if all men recognize the law of bread labour and also place their talents, whether moral or material, whether self-acquired or inherited, according to the existing laws of inheritance, at the disposal of the community for common human welfare.[20]

Gandhi, however, propounds his theory of Natural Law in the context of domestic society and evolves many doctrines viz., the doctrine of "the inner voice", the 'Satyagraha', 'Non-cooperation Movement', 'Satya, Ahimsa, Trusteeship, Sarvodaya, Gram-raj, Ramraj' etc.

There is no single instance in our knowledge in which Gandhi applied these doctrines himself in the international context. Most of his campaigns were undertaken in national context. No one is sure whether these techniques can be mechanically repeated in international situations. However, Gandhian notion of natural law of the essential human unity provides an answer to the threat of total human annihilation on the globe by nuclear holocaust. The problem of survival from nuclear holocaust is not merely a problem faced by nations, it is a problem faced by each man and woman on the earth. The nation-state system can not save them. On the contrary 'people' of the nation-state are left to suffer consequences of the blunders and misdeeds of their national leaders. Under the circumstances, the nations can not unite people. Only 'people' have to unite themselves, as Gandhi's notion reminds us that we share the whole humanity and not artificially created nation-states.

The message Gandhi left for us, in the international context, is that 'people' of the world have to organize themselves, in addition to the organization of nation-states. The nation-states do not even promisc the survival of its citizens which is its primary duty. Under such circumstances, if the mankind does not organize itself in an alternative way, international politics will degenerate into an oligopoly. There will be competitions amongst powerful nations to establish hegemony over weaker nations of the world. The building of alternative organization and fostering of co-operation following Gandhi's philosophy of Natural Law is the first step in the direction of achieving permanent ally of peace. Through his conception of 'natural law' Gandhi puts forward a universally recognized functional reality which has undisputed logic of its operation and, therefore, the strength of his argument is not his own. He only interprets it in his words and that is open for all other states to accept, yet difficult to reject.

Gandhi on War, and Justice

According to the political school of world order, the main cause of the outbreak of war is break-down in the present international order. Gandhi goes beyond this and asks why the so-called break down takes place. He does not blame the nation-state system. He blames lack of righteousness on the part of national leaders. According to Gandhi, greed, urge to exploit individuals and opportunities and desire to dominate them are the root causes of outbreak of war. Gandhi, therefore, opposes aggression, whether or not, it directly employs military force and receives legal recognition from the concerned parties or from international community. He always disapproves collective security system in order to prevent war mainly because it employs 'military force'. According to Gandhi one force confronting another can not create peace. In this way, peace can never be achieved by force. On the contrary the use of 'force' gets legitimized, in such a system.

Ideologically, Gandhi blames western imperialism, fascism and communism as serious threats to world peace and as causes war. Besides these political forces, he views man's economic greed and recourse to violence as deeper sources of aggression.[21] International ideologies driven by diplomacy, propaganda or subversion sometimes cause havoc in internal affairs of other nations. Hence, Gandhi condemns those ideologies and economic, political and military practices generated out of them, because they lead to inter-state conflicts or threaten world peace.

Economic Causes of War

Gandhi interprets colonialism and war in economic terms. While commenting on the British East India Company, Gandhi wrote in 1909 that its object was to increase its commerce and to make money. He further declared that once British imperialism was established, it would maintain arms, chiefly to protect its commerce.[22] He, thus, blames "exploitative colonialism as the first cause of war".[23] He claims that, European Powers fought chiefly to redistribute colonial spoils.

Gandhi on International Treaties

International order operates through two devices. First, it operates either through the systems of balance of power, balance of terror; or through the principle of deterrence (non-use of nuclear power). Second device especially advocated by Bull, maintains that state system survives through customs, conventions, agreements or treaties. According to Gandhi, both these devices are not adequate enough to maintain order in international society. To Gandhi, international treaties and agreements are just patchworks for survival. It is not a lasting solution, either to make it function permanently or to turn it into a world order system based on human consideration.

The turbulent period of Indian freedom struggle, which Gandhi lived and led, was the period between the two world wars. This period gave birth to many international treaties in order to keep the international order going somehow. Gandhi charges openly the Allied Power after the victory in the first world war that they did not have intention either to improve the international order or to create the world order based on justice. The case, he quotes, is that of the Versailles Peace Treaty (1919). In his opinion, it was "a treaty of revenge against Germany by the victors",[24] at the conclusion of World War I. He observes, "If the terms (of the 1919 peace treaties) which are announced had been described as the terms of war, the description would have been truer to facts".[25]

In his view, forced peace is not a true peace. It is a violation of truth. Peace can never be imposed from without, it should flourish from within. Peace concluded through war is not real peace; it is at best a patched-up situation resulting from mutual exhaustion. It can not create a new order. Gandhi regrets that the Allied Powers did not show understanding or consideration for Germany in the Versailles treaty. He predicted that the (the first world) war which was greater than the *Mahabharat* war was just a prelude to a still greater war...He further said, "if the defeat of Germany and the Central Powers ended the German peril, the victory of the Allies had brought into a period no less deadly to the peace of the world.[26] While commenting on the Second World War he wrote: "the War will end this year or next, it will bring victory to the Allies. The pity of it is that it will be only so-called.... That victory will be assuredly a prelude to a deadlier war...[27]

While commenting on the treaty with Turkey, Gandhi described the treaty as a "monument of human arrogance and man-made injustice... is a triumph not of humanity but a demonstration of inhumanity".[28] Gandhi rejected the Kellogg-Briand Pact (of August 1928) as a peace move, as by that pact, the signatories were to announce war as an instrument of national policy. Gandhi dubbed it as a device "to carry on the joint exploitation peacefully", and described it as another attempt to preserve status quo. With regard to the Munich Pact, Gandhi said that it merely postponed the war, "the danger of war has been averted for the time being". Gandhi believed, "it marked Hitler's personal triumph of violence".[29] While commenting on the Munich Pact, after a decade, Gandhi described it as "peace without honour", and "Europe has sold her soul for the sake of a seven days earthly existence".[30] Gandhi condemned the secret treaties signed during the first world war, as he saw that they could not ensure peace. According to him, it was a convenient arrangement for achieving a particular objective. The signatories were not serious about it, and they even considered, "their own written word as to much waste paper".[31] He disapproved the German-Soviet Pact of August 23, 1939 as an "unnatural combination of the two countries".[32]

Thus, Gandhi had no faith in bilateral peace treaties concluded by any two or more countries. All these treaties, according to him,, were motivated to serve selfish, narrow national interests and to buy time for future possible war. Gandhi says, "peace must be just and in order to be that, it must neither be punitive nor vindictive.... The fruit of peace must equally be shared".[33]

Gandhi realized that either bilateral arrangement (Peace Treaties), or multinational arrangement through a type of international institution (League of Nation) might help in perpetuating international order. But, this international order was not worth as it was based on injustice and exploitation of the weak by the strong. Such a status-quo would work in favour of the Allied powers and all efforts were directed in preserving that status-quo. For Gandhi, this type of international order can neither yield peace nor preserve it. It can not create an atmosphere for disarmament or internationalism.

Gandhi's Concept of Justice in World Politics

This section provides an abstract on Gandhi's thinking on justice in three parts: First, it inquires Gandhi's meaning of justice in world politics; second, it analyses how far Gandhi related 'order' to justice; and third, to what extent, Gandhi thinks order and justice as conflicting concepts and what is his priority? All these three are treated simultaneously.

Gandhian Meaning of Justice Within International Order (Inter-State Justice)

General Definition of Justice

Gandhi's concept of 'justice' embodied '*Sarvodaya*' ("the good of all") as against the maximum good of the maximum people. It is a plea for concern and consideration for the good of the down-trodden or the most neglected man. Gandhi knows that "an ideal is never fully realized in life".[34] It is an ideal, a glorious distant goal which one should strive to achieve. Gandhi takes it as a reference point which indicate to man a direction rather than the destination. In order to realize the goal of *sarvodaya*, a predominantly non-violent society — internal, and international and world societies — need to be created.

Inter-State Justice

Gandhi's '*sarvodaya*' refers to the good for all states in an international society irrespective of any consideration. In order to create an international society, he pleads for "economic justice", sovereign equality, and peaceful cooperation among states as requisites for international harmony. He visualizes that the present international order is based on injustice as economic injustice is endemic in international society under the domination of western colonialism. Strong nations exploit weak ones and the weak are at the receiving ends. According to Gandhi, 'peace' can be preserved in international society provided it backs the idea of self-determination of most peoples. Gandhi stands for the rules of morality which confers rights and duties upon states and nations. He advocates that all states, irrespective of their size, or racial composition, or ideological leaning, are entitled to equal rights of sovereignty. He pleads for the idea that all nations are also entitled to equal rights of national self-determination.[35]

In international society, the main participators are 'states'. Hence, the state becomes the main focus of everyday discussion of justice in world affairs. Gandhi agreed to the idea of General Justice in international society as he believed that every state does not have only rights and duties in legal terms but also has moral duties to perform. It has to ensure that its policy remains morally correct. He supports the claim of equality or fairness in treatment between India and other states, or between defeated nations and victorious ones. He pleads specifically for substantive justice by which he claims moral right to sovereignty or independence for all the states in the world. He asserts the right of equal treatment among states of the world, specifically in voting in international assembly. This is because India and other colonies were denied right to vote in the League of Nations, Thus, he also stands for arithmetical justice. Gandhi often argues out his case for justice from the point of view of a common good of the world community while pleading for distributive justice. He, thus, deals with all sorts of justice in society.

Gandhi pleads for generous attitude to be adopted by the Allied Powers to the vanquished ones, while concluding peace treaties. He never conceives a world which has to live under the fear of bomb. Big nations, by monopolizing atomic weapons, blackmail weak nations. This is a part of injustice. He declared that no nation can bully others and no nation should live in fear. Unless this is ensured, justice can not be resorted.

Gandhi propagates inter-state fellowship and good will. He has great conviction in *dharmic* law (law of living) which imposes moral obligation on states, as well as on individuals. He advocates that disputes should be settled amicably at the level of the parties concerned. Orientation of justice, according to him, is based on the idea of 'one world' incorporating the ideals of "truth" and "non-violence".

Justice and War

Gandhi witnessed many small and big wars during his life span. He even participated in the Boer and the Zulu wars as a non-combatant soldier during his stay in South Africa. The two World Wars were fought when he was at the center-stage of national politics of India. In the First World War, he even recruited soldiers for the British Empire. On every occasion, Gandhi expressed his views on war.[36] From the Boer War to the Indo-Pak War on Kashmir, on many such occasions, Gandhi proclaimed that war is evil, nevertheless he maintained that "under exceptional circumstances war may have to be resorted to as a necessary evil".[37]

Gandhi maintains that in a war 'justice' goes with one of the two sides. War can therefore, enable justice to triumph. He writes, "If the motive is right it (war) can be turned to the profit of mankind and that an '*ahimsaist*' may not stand aside and look on with indifference, but, must make his choice and actively co-operate or actively resist".[38] However, he showed strong and clear preference to resist, he showed strong and clear preference to resist war by non-violent means, the total *satyagraha.* But if a nation is not trained in the nonviolent resistance, or does not know the techniques of it, it can even resist it with violence. He prefers violent resistance in war to coward submission to the aggressor. To him, "all killing is not *hinsa*".[39]

Gandhi considers war a vital activity that no nation can remain neutral or detached from. He categorically states that if we live in a state and procure all benefits from it (food, protection, etc.) it becomes our duty as a citizen to defend the state. Neutrality, in such case, is an escapism or cheating oneself from within. Justifying his participation in war he once stated, "The choice before me was only that either we must renounce the benefits of the state or help it to the best of our ability".[40] Gandhi told pacifists that adopting intellectual neutrality during wartime is always indefensible. No matter how much they detest violence, they must decide which is the just side in a violence, they must decide which is the just side in a military contest.[41]

In short, Gandhi never believed that war is the absence of justice. He however, maintains that peace is superior to war in all respects. He also believes that war is in - built in the nation-state system and, therefore, it breaks out every now and then. Although war is cruel and brutalizing the mankind, it is related to justice to the extent that it is a adopted by the parties to realize justice. Gandhi, however, never agrees that war is the method to bring about justice.[42]

Atomic Weapons and Justice

War is fought, according to Gandhi, in order to achieve justice. War may not be rational or national in nature. But it is instrumental to achieve justice. With whatever words, we may condemn war. However, it is fought to win in order to get justice. One side must win and other must loose. War is not meant for total destruction. War is not massacre. Echoing this feeling Gandhi states that use of nuclear weapons can never be 'just', and nothing of value results from an atomic war. Gandhi believes that war has no relations to justice which can be ascertained from the Atomic warfare. He once said: "so far as I can see, the atom bomb has deadened the finest feeling that has sustained mankind for ages. There used to be the so-called laws of war which made it tolerable. Now we know naked truth. War knows no law except that of might". In short, Gandhi does not believe that Atomic war can't be fought for justice.[43]

It must be borne in mind that for Gandhi, war is not justifiable *per se*, but 'justice' is in war as one side can always be justified to wage a war. War may be condemned, but we can not remain neutral when it is thrust upon us. One has to take the side which ever he finds favouring justice and participate in it. One may participate to win it, or restrict it or to lessen the damage of it. One has to participate in it because in today's world you are involved in it directly or indirectly. You are a citizen of a state hence you are under the obligation of a state to fight. You, therefore, must fight. Even if you do not fight physically, you participate in it passively by paying tax to the state. War is an activity which does not permit luxury of neutrality. So to participate in it in either way, actively or passively; or directly or indirectly is justice.

Gandhi on Justice in World Order

The idea of justice in society of men relates to what is right and good for the mankind as a whole. It differs from the notion of what is good for the society of states whose constituent member is sovereign state. The notion of world justice concerns what is good for the universal society of mankind whose constituent members are individual - human beings. In the present day world politics, the problem of nuclear disaster, transfer of resources from the poor to the rich countries, or the problem of environment are considered in terms of the solidarity of human beings. The appeal is made not for cooperation among states, but basically for the solidarity of all human beings who face that challenge as human beings. The mankind is divided among sovereign states. As a result, they don't have the means of interest-articulation or political socialization and recruitment which are the hallmarks of apolitical system. We are interested to find out what Gandhi has to say on this situation. At present, we articulate our interest only through the society of states and international organizations.

Gandhi opines that, justice in a society for mankind can be achieved provided the mankind gives up hunger for wealth and greedy pursuit of worldly pleasures. His central concept of justice is, thus, related to the concept of modern man as a 'selfish creature". To pursue self interest is considered a virtue by the modern civilization.

Philosophically, he believes that, basically men are spiritually united to each other and this transcends their temporal differences. But essentially, a spiritual man has become a materialist man, who is guided chiefly by self-interests. He wants to and strives to acquire resources at the cost of other's interests.[44] The excessive concern for pursuit of self-interest creates a mismatch between private and public morality. It also affects adversely the edifice of social obligations and co-operation. In this context, the role of violence has been significant. Gandhi calls it a civilizational crisis. Once, pursuit of self-interest becomes central in life, the higher values of life such as spirituality, morality, justice, etc. get crowded in individual's life.[45]

Modern civilization which justifies pursuit of self-interest, as natural and rational considers restrictions on individual's life as hindrance to the development of the personality of individual. The centrality of the pursuit of self-interest makes expediency, rather than morality, the basis of interpersonal and intergroup relations.

Justice in the society of mankind can be resorted to, provided 'morality is restored as the basis of interpersonal relations. The restoration of ethics and morality in private and public life of mankind can bring back spiritual unity among all men. Gandhi believes that his own principles are reflections of this unity and they are universally applicable in the visible world.[46] The restoration of spiritual unity is 'truth', to Gandhi, to be realized by every one. Gandhi holds truth as the ultimate good, not peace. It means, once the truth is realized, justice will follow automatically and society will be full of peace and justice. In the Gandhian scheme, truth, justice and peace are interrelated. Nevertheless justice is given priority over peace. Gandhi never wants peace at the cost of truth or justice.

Gandhi wants that, mankind should implement principles of self-help, self-reliance, simple living, high thinking, *satyagrah*, non-violence, trusteeship, *swadesi, swarajya* etc. in the world society. Justice will follow it. Gandhi does not demand any type of integration — political, economic or cultural — in order to realize justice in International Relations.[47]

In his conception of justice, Gandhi's focal point is man, but he wants to reconstruct the live world with the help of his principles, The key element in this reconstruction is the return to the idea of man forming an essential part of a larger order, spiritual order.

Gandhi further views that the success of the world order does not depend on empowering of man by coercive powers. It certainly depends on the extent to which he values morals and establishes relations with eternal world on the basis of certain ethical norms. It is sheer arrogance on the part of man if he regards himself as superior to existing laws of beings. He is as much a part of cosmos as any other living or non-living being.

Justice and Order

Justice and order are interrelated and they impinge upon each other especially in the international society. According to Gandhi, 'justice' can never be obtained in the existing international order as it is based on violence and exploitation. It helps to create the domination of the big military powers over small nations. The imperialist structure of power in Gandhi's time was based on 'injustice' and the Great Powers (England, France) wanted to perpetuate that status-quo. Hence, 'justice', in terms of equality of nations, and eradication of racialism and exploitation was just a dream. Hence, the order needed to be changed.

The international order is based on the principle of deterrence. This means reliance on violence and weapons of violence. These weapons (including nuclear) threaten uprooting of the value systems of all nations. How can justice be preserved when all the nations have to operate under threat? Under the circumstances, no other value system except 'threat' and 'terror' by nuclear blackmail can prevail.

From the point of view of human civilization Gandhi is a severe critic of the British civilization. He described India's anti-colonial struggle as a conflict between the Indian civilization and the British civilization. The British system was based on the value system of dominance, inequality and fear. Gandhi thought that unless the foundations of this civilization is changed, no justice can prevail. Gandhi, therefore, calls for change in the value system of an industrialized power in general.[48]

Gandhi recognizes an inherent conflict between the values of order and of justice in world politics, and thinks that 'justice' should be given priority. He fought against the British, not only to achieve freedom for India, but also to re-establish basic human value. Moreover, Gandhi was all the time demanding decolonization once and for all; so that the order based on 'injustice' could be rectified. Besides, Gandhi demanded 'equal treatment' for all the nations within and without the League of Nations. He further demanded that, all the nations should be granted economic equality from the imperialist powers after sovereign equality being granted to them; so that the exploitation of the weak by the strong could be prevented.

Gandhi fought for India's independence with non-violent means. His struggle intended to subordinate order to 'justice' because, that order was prescribed by the British Imperialism and was based on 'violence'. Finally, Gandhi succeeded in creating a consensus in international society as a whole in favour of a change in terms of decolonization. Thus, without submitting to the 'order' based on violence Gandhi fought for 'justice' from the platform of non-violence.

In the society of mankind (world order), Gandhi prioritizes 'Man' because, according to him justice can prevail provided the dignity of human being is maintained in the world order. Gandhi presumes that cosmic spiritual order is already there. It has been disturbed by Man himself as he is driven by self-interest. Man has become 'immoral' and enemy of himself. Gandhi, however, stands for reconstruction of that order in a world of living, with the help of man. The key element in this reconstruction is the return to the idea of Man, forming an essential part of a large order.

Gandhi views order as an objective reality. It is a cosmic order. It is governed by certain norms and sustained by *dharma* (law of living). It is inherent in the very nature of things. That order can be sustained only when each individual contributes in his own way to the preservation of that order by shaping his life activities through thinking and action, in accordance with the cosmic law.[49]

According to Gandhi, man in the present world has refrained from the cosmic law. Hence the order is disturbed. Man's such indifference has two reasons: (1) he has become selfish; and (2) he has forgotten that all of us have emerged from one center, hence all of us are related to each other. This realization helps the human being to explore the inner depths of his being and initiates the process of self-transformation.

Justice is not maintained in the world order because, that the cosmic order is disturbed by man himself. Hence, we need to imbibe truth and nonviolence and other values in order to restore that order. This projects a universalistic outlook. Along with it, a concrete path for articulating and realizing these universal values need be chosen.

Gandhi does not advocate homogenization of a world society. He wants that each individual should not tie up his own cultural heritage. He believes that only by proceeding from wherever we are, we can make an integral effort required for the progress and peace of the humanity. The dignity of an individual can be maintained if the above-mentioned situation is encouraged in the society to mankind.

Gandhi has different interpretation of justice in international society and in world society. His priority is 'justice' rather than 'order'. He criticized prevailing unjust order and struggled against it but, by non-violent means. Gandhi sometimes treats war as having connection with justice, which relegates peace as such to a subordinate level. Peace based on injustice is not real peace for Gandhi. It is a peace of a grave yard. Gandhi stands for dynamic, just and peaceful order in international society as well as in the world society.

Individual : Another Component of International Society

Another equally important component of the international society, as Gandhi views, is the individual. Gandhi accords equal importance to individuals as individuals together run the nation-state system. They form the 'state' and now they ought to form a world federation (super state) out of the nation-state system. He even wants individuals to sacrifice their life for the benefit of the world. Referring to the place and duty of the individuals in a global hierarchy, Gandhi writes, "Just as the cult of patriotism teaches us today that the individual has to die for the family, the village for the district, the district for the province, and the province for the country, even so a country has to be free in order that it may die, if necessary, for the benefit of the world".[50]

Man

Man, as an individual by nature, according to Gandhi, is good, but he has become idle and indifferent to the purpose for which the state is created. The state is created for truth and non-violence, but it has become a house of violence. The state should serve Man but Man has become subservient to state. In other words, Man must be the master of a state, but state in turn has become the master of Man. The duty of an individual towards the state is conditional on the degree to growth and welfare. But, an individual forgets this. Consequently, the state emerged to operate internally as a mechanism of dominance to which the people must submit or suffer. The state has brought Man to his feet to serve it and the society of Man had failed to check the power of the state. It had failed to hold the state responsible for the welfare of the individual. Society must restrain and control the state. But it is not so. As a result, the state has become soulless and unresponsive to human feelings and emotions. If the state behaviour continues to be like this, it is never likely to be stripped-off its coercive power to which it owes its existence. Gandhi's words defining the relation between the state and an individual - echo in J.S. Mills', "State is a necessary evil and individual has to function within the bounds of 'self-regarding and other regarding activities' ". Here 'self-regarding' devotes individual's role and 'other regarding' stands for the state. The question is; whether the state exists for the individual or the individual exists for the state? It is in this inevitable context that both, Gandhi and Mill, accommodate the state out of sheer necessity and compulsion. The state would be obsolete, provided human nature reform itself to that state or position.

Gandhi regard the individual as the center of authority. The state and the government derive their existence and power form individual. Their object should, therefore, be to help the all-round evolution of individual by enacting and enforcing law, by preventing problems and by ensuring security, peace and progress to individuals. The state should always hold high the spirit of service and should never behave like the master of the people.[51]

Gandhi wants that state should gradually and eventually become a welfare institution, less and less coercive and cautious. Speaking of his ideal of the state Gandhi says, "There is then a state of enlightened anarchy. In such a state one is one's own ruler. He rules himself in such a manner that he is never a hindrance to his neighbour..."[52]

Gandhi believes that when an individual learns to rule himself (*swaraj*), he develops fully. He, then, develops moral and social senses naturally. His cultivated moral and social senses further help him to develop love for humanity which would break all national and geographical barriers.

Hence, an international Man as per Gandhian conception is no one else but an extension of a 'national Man'. In this way, Gandhi does not see any tension between nationalism and internationalism. Gandhian nationalism draws its inspiration from the dominant Indian belief in the fundamental unity of humanity in spite of diversity, and the consequent belief in the reasonableness of human equality. So nationalism logically leads on to internationalism.

Gandhi says, "My notion of *Purna Swaraj*" (i.e., complete self-rule) is not isolated independence but healthy and dignified interdependence". Moreover, "our nationalism can be no peril to other nations in as much as we will exploit none just as we will allow none to exploit us. Through swaraj we would serve the whole world.[53]

Gandhi's Transforming Strategy and Nation-States

Gandhi, does not agree with the present efforts of creating international institutions like the League of Nations and the United Nations Organization (UNO) for the solution of the problem of war. He suggests to set up a World Federation of nation-state to turn the nation-state system into a society. On two grounds, he objects to the creation of the international institution to solve the problem of war. Firstly, this institution (UNO) has been founded to safeguard the interests of the powers who created them. And secondly, violence is the basic principle applied to maintain peace in the world. Gandhi is convinced that peace can never be preserved by violent means. His views will be discussed, one by one, in the following pages. He evolves a non-violent and constitutional scheme to reorganize the entire international society based on the principles of mutual understanding and mutual help.

Gandhi on International Institutions : Supranationalism

According to Gandhi, the League of Nations or the United Nations Organizations (UNO) can not further the ideal of one world as they are not universal institutions. After the Second World War, when the Great Powers were deliberating on the creation of the United Nations Organization (UNO), Gandhi asserted, "If they are so arrogant as to think that they can have lasting peace while the exploitation of the coloured and the so-called backward races goes on, they are living in fool's paradise".[54] Gandhi firmly believes that the League and the UNO are the product of war and not the positive manifestations of the natural urge of nations for peace. These institutions were the outcome of - lust, anger, fear, mistrust, selfishness and compromise. Gandhi, therefore, thinks that they are not capable to preserve or promote peace. Such institutions can not remove war from the body politic of the international society.

Gandhi, in fact, maintains that the only thing the UNO can do is to legitimize the use of force by the device like the collective security system. Gandhi is convinced that war is certainly not the way to tackle inter-state disputes. To Gandhi, Violence can never be met with violence. He wonders how such an institutions can give birth to the idea of oneness or equality among the nations of the international society.

In order to remove the feeling of insecurity and fear, and to lessen the degree of exploitation in the present international order, Gandhi proposes the idea of a world government through federation of nation-states based on equality.

World Government through World Federation

The ultimate objective of Gandhi is to create a world government. But, initially he suggests that 'World Federation', a federations of all the sovereign nations should have the base of the main principle of non-violence, "I may not get a World Government that I want just now, but it is a government that would just touch my ideal. I would accept it as a compromise. Therefore, although I am not enamoured of a world federation I shall be prepared to accept it, if it is built on essentially non-violent basis".[55]

Being a realist, Gandhi knows that the nation-state will not give - up their sovereignty totally and at once. The sovereignty is very much dear to them. But some how, he is convinced that they (Nations) could be persuaded to part with it partially. Hence, Gandhi prefers to have first a federation as an immediate institution aiming which may be gradually converted into the world government. He is sure that all the nation-states will agree to have federation because they are afraid of each other. Secondly, they feel isolated, and thirdly, Gandhi thinks, the common people strive for this type of federation. The nation-states, even otherwise are interdependent and, in Gandhi's opinion, the federation will bring about friendly inter-dependence. The friendly inter-dependent will be more acceptable to the nation-states than the forced one.

Dissolution of Empire and Formation of Federation

It was easier, Gandhi thought in 1920s, to form a world federation then. The entire world was then divided into empires; viz. the British empire; the French Empire; the Russian Empire and the most of the people of Asia-Africa were not independent nations. the Afro-Asian nations have not yet tasted the fruit of sovereignty. Gandhi feared that they would not agree to give-up their (Afro-Asian Nations) sovereignty if they tasted it once. Hence, he suggested to turn the "Empire System" into a "World Federation System" as it was easier to do so... empire idea dissolves and the world state takes its place in which all the states of the world are free and equal, no state has its military.[56]

Gandhi puts three conditions for the formation of federation: first, freedom of all nations, irrespective of whether conquered and exploited ones; second, to recognize the axis of powers immediately after the war ends, as members of the world federation should keep army of its own; third, it should be a non-violent army (or policy). These are necessary conditions otherwise the federation will fall to pieces under the slightest strains.[57]

Mini-experiment of Federation

To operationalize the idea of federation, Gandhi advocated to turn the institution of the British commonwealth into that of a federation. It was easy to do so and would be a logical step to the world federation. He stood for transformation of the commonwealth. He advocated to transmit it into a "fellowship of free nations joined together by the "Silver code of love". He wanted India to join it, as he maintained that "my ambition is much higher than independence"[58] of India.

No Federation Through the League or the UNO

Unlike the commonwealth, the other international institutions, according to Gandhi were based on the "force". The intention of the founder of the League was hypocritical. In his letter to C.P. Andrews, he chided President Wilson when he tried to justify the use of force through the League of Nations. Gandhi wrote: "If the moral pressure... failed, the members of the League would not hesitate to use the last remedy, viz., brute force".[59]

The heart of the League of Nations is the system of collective security system. It is based on the principle of "one for all and all for one". But when it failed to translate that system against the Japanese aggression on Manchuria in 1931, Gandhi reflected that it was a mere device of the League to serve the national interests of the Great Powers. Gandhi considers the League only an institution to pursue national interests of the few by other means, "What is the League of Nations? Is it not in realty merely England and France? Do other powers count? Is it any use appealing to France which is denying her motto of fraternity, equality and justice?"[60]

While commenting on the Syrian problem, Gandhi held that there was no sense, or use, in making appeals to these organizations, for they were entirely unable to do justice as they have double standards in its application. Advising Abyassinians, he said not to appeal to the League. He wrote : "The League is expected to perform wonders. It is expected to replace war and by its own power arbitrate between nations who might have differences between themselves. But it has always seemed to me that the League lacks the necessary sanction. It depends as it has to, largely if not exclusively, on the judgment of the nations concerned".[61]

Gandhi knows that the conflict is inevitable in international society. Nations are going to pursue their national interests, hence, there are chances for incompatibility of interests. At such times, the League is expected to arbitrate between the disputant parties. But, Gandhi expressed his doubt about the future of the League, when it was first conceived by President Wilson. Its composition, which was marked by the only two dominant powers namely U.K. and France, disillusioned him. The Asyassinian and Manchurian crisis shattered Gandhi's last hope in the international institutions and their capacity to turn it into a world federation.

As we have seen, Gandhi does not put faith in exclusivist, expansionist nationalism. He has also lost faith in the institutions of the League and the UNO based on supra-nationalism. In fact the idea of supra-nationalism facilitates relatively great co-operation and possible understanding, Gandhi now becomes disillusioned with supra-nationalism as it has turned to be means to dominate and exploit others. Gandhi expresses great resentment against these institutions because they legitimize use of brute force under the guise of the collective security system.

As we have seen, Gandhi is even against the collective security system to preserve peace. Then, what alternative does Gandhi suggest to the collective security system to preserve peace among nations even when the aggression takes place? As pointed out, Gandhi advocates that the nation-state system was not bad, only its operation was dangerous, as it was organized on the principle of violence. Now, it has developed nuclear teeth. Hence, Gandhi advocates the pulling out teeth of the nuclear weapons giving up violence and making the world ready for world federation.

In spite of the fact that the nation-state system gives up armaments some sort of arms will remain. The nation-state will perhaps abolish nuclear weapons and the conventional disarmament may also be implemented. Yet, a nation will commit aggression on another nation by non-lethal weapons like lathi, stone etc. How would Gandhi resist such an aggression? He suggests the following technique to treat the aggressor. It could be divided into three parts:

1. The Plan for Action Before Invasion Takes Place

First of all, Gandhi suggests removal of the probable causes or motives behind a possible invasion. According to him, suppose if the motive is economic, that is, the satisfaction of primary needs, one should encourage them to be economically self-reliant. Thus, Gandhi suggests to implement the principle of helpful neighbourhood, that is, 'live and let live' in the field of International Relations. Indirectly, it is a plea for free dissemination of ideas and knowledge. He teaches extension of human sympathy to all the people of the world. Done in a purer spirit, as advocated by Gandhi, it is likely to yield increasing returns. This is a non-violent way of removing the probable causes of invasion.

2. The Plan to be Adopted During the Period of Armed Attack

He suggests that "fighting" against the aggressor should "firstly" be non-violent. He wants to fight to the last man without any bitterness or hatred against the invader. He presumes that the aggressor will be tired of killing non-violent resisters, mentally and physically. He will begin to search for a new force which refuses co-operation with him and yet, desists from "hurting". This will probably desist from further slaughter. He, thus, wants to weaken the morale of the aggressor. He says, 'pure *Ahimsa* or sufferings is self-propagating'. The invader, even if invisible is sure to be softened and influenced by it. In any case, by such sufferings, 'the resisters' will gain the good will in the entire world.

In the second stage, Gandhi suggests that one may defend even violently, if he does not believe or has no faith in non-violent technique. In any case, he does not favour surrendering in a cowardly manner. He emphasizes that even violent resistance may be done with the point of performing duty.

Even in violent warfare, Gandhi advises the minimum possible use of violence and force. He announces his position against the policy of scorched earth, sabotage and secrecy.

3. The Attitude to be Adopted During the Occupation of Territories by the Invaders

The attitude needs to be taken with the aggressor, as described by Gandhi, is that of "non-violent non-cooperation". He is of the opinion that, if there is a total non-cooperation by the conquered nation, the invader is bound to withdraw, sooner or later, in sheer disgust and confusion. One can draw a parallel between the British invasion of India with that of an aggressor's occupation. To protect it, Gandhi resorted to non-violent, non-cooperation techniques - though it did require immeasurable courage and tolerance on the part of resisters. Despite India's ultimate independence. the British held no ill-will against Gandhi.

It is a unique technique but every individual who resides in a nation needs to be a true *satyagrahi* in the Gandhian sense.[62] Gandhi suggests that an individual needs to be trained to be a true *satyagrahi.* Satyagrahi soldier is a brave and courageous man. He should not be a coward. *Ahimsa* is for a fearless man. To practice, it requires a courage of conviction.

Every time war does not break out between the nations, but it is incompatibility of national interests that gives birth to the conflicts between nations. Now, let us see what technique Gandhi suggests to resolve conflicts between nations.

Gandhi's Technique of Conflict Resolution Under the Shadow of Nuclear Threat

So long as Nation-State System does not give way to the world government, conflicts will perpetuate under state-system. Gandhi, therefore, suggests a technique of resolving conflicts in which vital interests of the nations are not involved and nuclear disarmament has not yet taken place.

Gandhi wants us to remember that "co-operation" and "harmony", rather than "conflict" and "struggle", are the fundamental laws of the universe. And there is a fundamental "unity" in the universe and society, which sustains *order* and *life*. Gandhi reminds us that Man does not live by destruction.

What is Conflict? How to Resolve it?

Gandhi views conflicts as temporary irregularities in the even flow of life. He believes that conflict can never be ceaseless phenomena in the universe. Therefore, the resolution of creative conflict to him means: (a) elimination of maladjustment; (b) progress towards a better and a more meaningful readjustment; and (c) transformation of violent relationship into a non-violent one. This means that energies of the opponents are to be integrated to achieve a higher goal.

While discussing the reasons for conflict, he does not blame 'individual antagonism, but blames the 'system'. To him, defective system is responsible for conflict. He does not regard antagonism between two individuals (or classes) responsible for it. Hence, in order to eliminate 'conflict', the system needs to be changed. The conflict between India and England was basically a conflict between the Indian national movement and the British System, and not between Indian and British individuals.

In order to change the system, Gandhi advocates the method of dialogue between the conflicting parties. he suggests social and constructive discourse between the conflicting parties which resolve into changing the system.[63]

According to Gandhi, violence/*himsa* is the root cause of conflict. He defines *Himsa* as (a) willful use of force in the traditional sense to compel one to do things which he would not do otherwise; (b) Using methods synonymous with moral evil in general: corruption, hypocrasy, falsehood, deceit, cowardice and hatred. He uses such methods in two ways: in behavioural sense and in mental sense.

Gandhi says no one can be an apostle of an absolute truth. Truth is always relative. Hence, a conflict always involves different views or relative truth. In order to resolve a conflict, therefore, these varied sets of relative truths need to be synthesized. It becomes an improvement upon one's position. It will be a progress towards the absolute truth. Thus, his perception of truth denies the employment of violence as a means to resolve a conflict.

The Gandhian technique of resolving conflicts differs from the traditional one on many counts: (a) it does not ask any party to sacrifice his positions; (b) It does not demand any concession; (c) There is no sense of victory or/defeat of one party over the other; and (d) All synthesis is a triumph for both the parties.

Conflict can't be resolved at a stroke. It is a gradual process. Joan

Bondurant classifies it into three stage.[64] Each stage should be taken up only after the failure of the preceding one.

Three Stages

1. **Persuasion** through reason or negotiation.
2. **Shock Therapy:** To persuade the opponent through self-suffering. It strengthens "Reason" and it opens the eyes of understanding (Shock Therapy).
3. **Non-Violent Direct Action :** It is characterized by tools such as non-cooperation and civil disobedience. It can be applied against government as well as against individuals or a group conflicts.

It may not be a full-proof technique. Even Gandhi himself never claims as a full proof one. But it is the most viable technique of resolving conflicts in a nuclear age.

Transforming Strategy for Man

The essential problem is how to create a community of men in the world so that conflicts and incompatibility between individual welfare and collective good can be resolved amicably. In order to achieve harmony in the world, Gandhi suggests to change the structure of international order and also pleads for cultivating self-control in individual, as well as his harmony with the environment, which consists of political power, community and eco-system.

Gandhi suggests a two-prong strategy for world order: (1) Re-socialization of Man and (2) Harmony between Power, Community and Eco-system. In working out these strategy effectively, he calls for spade work at the grass-root level.

Re-socialization of Man

In working out this strategy, Gandhi views 'order' itself as the point of departure as it forms an integral part of Man's being and becomes the ground for both self-development and social harmony. An individual and his transformation is the central issue of Gandhian thinking. Basically, Gandhi wants to resocialise Man through self-discipline and through the system of basic education based on the twin principles of 'dialogue' and 'involvement' of man with man with total involvement of 'heart', 'head' and 'hand'.

Gandhi's philosophy of re-socializing man is based on a simple of assumptions: first, Man can be taken as what he ought to be, and not necessarily as what he really is. A desirable change in Man's character can be brought about, not only by refashioning institutions (environment) surrounding him, but also by reforming Man himself.[65]

Secondly, Man himself is a part of order and not the world order only. It is a larger order, which forms an integral part of Man's being and becomes the ground for both self-development and social harmony. This order considers Man as a starting point of any project of reconstruction of the living world.[66] It is inconceivable to compartmentalize 'order' (world) at state or even at individual level and, therefore, Gandhi's conception of order is not based on 'Man vs Nature' or 'Man vs World'. Man is incorporated in the scheme of order, whether the state or the world. The organic unity of Man and the universe needs to be realized.

The present world is governed by certain norms and sustained by an order necessary for its preservation. The order is an objective one, inherent in the very nature of things. This order is sustained by *Dharma* - law of living - which regulates the working of the cosmos and keeps it in the proper course. It signifies both the governance and regulation of the physical aspects of the cosmos as well as moral order.[67]

What is Self-Transformation ?

It is directly connected with transcending individual's, or state's self-interest. In order to transcend the motive self-interest, one has to perceive himself as the ethico-religious man, and not as bio/psycho/sociological man. Secondly, one must conceive that an individual is a part of a larger whole - a universal community. It is on the basis of this two-fold realization that one can, as Gandhi puts it, "share the majesty of life in the presence of God". This is possible if one rises above the phenomenal and explores the inner depths of one's being. This exploration initiates the process of self-transformation.[68]

The process of self-transformation must take place in this world. The world is essential for self-development and it has to be reshaped in the image of freedom and morality one seeks to attain on one's own life.

A transformed individual will shed the Promethean attitude on the external world and he will emphasize an essential relatedness of all creation. This transformed self widens the circle of community to include those who are currently excluded by separate states.[69] Simultaneously, it also stands for promotion of social and political relations within the boundaries of existing societies.

Gandhi here, redefines relations between 'self' and 'others'. To a transformed self, 'others' cease to be objects separated from the self and become in essence extended selves. Harmony with an ever-enlarging circle of relationships constitutes a personal aspiration, social goal and cosmic ideal.

The Gandhian orientation of transformation changes the definition of society. To Gandhi, society becomes an extended self rather than a mechanical aggregate of enclosed selves. This image of society locates humanity in a complex web of interdependency. Gandhi is also aware of the fact that no society is wholly composed of persons engaged in the process of self-transformation.[70]

Gandhi also emphasizes *ahimsa* (non-violence) as a fundamental outlook on life. Commitment of truth and acceptance of ahimsa foster an organismic vision based on the clear recognition that no one individual has a privileged access to truth. The development of true individuality must occur, not through a willful conquest of others, but through harmonizing oneself with an ever expanding network of harmonious, interdependent and cooperative relationships. It is this pattern of self-development that instills rationality and morality in the individual. They can not be instilled from any external source, hence individual himself has to change.[71]

The idea of self-transformation is related to the idea of "*swaraj*" advocated by Gandhi. *Swarajya* (self-rule) enables man to resist exploitation and oppression. It will prompt them to fight for what they believe in. As Gandhi points out, real *swaraj* is experienced, not by acquisition of authority by a few, but by acquisition of capability by all to resist authority when it is abused.[72]

The second dimension of Gandhian thinking is his system of Basic Education. He assigns to the non-violent state, a duty to educate the people. He wants ethical education to occupy the first place.[73] The basic aim of the education should be to make "men of us" and "enable us to do our duty". Character-building should be the aim of true education.[74] Hence, disciplining individuals is an essential part of education. He writes, "I would feel that if we succeed in building the character of the individual, society will take care of itself. I would be quite willing to trust the organization of society to individuals so developed".[75] Gandhi wants that a child should be taught through manual training and craft work, and not only through text books. The handicraft should also be taught in a "scientific manner" and not mechanically.

The literary education also figures in the syllabi, and subjects like Indian history and Indian geography are to be taught in the light of world history and world geography. The aim is to eliminate any tendency to narrow and rapid nationalism which can be a hindrance to cooperation and peace. Gandhi, thus, suggests a peace-oriented education scheme. Gandhi's way to peaceful world order is through education of right type of subjects and self-discipline.

Harmony Between Power and Community

Gandhi realizes that the 'self-interest' is the primary goal of man and, however, a man may be self-disciplined order can not be achieved as long as it remains so. Besides, the realization of common goods depends on self-control, not so much on the part of the individual, as on the part of the authority external to man. It is more so in the international society in which, 'state' is going to take decision on behalf of individuals. Hence, it is not only necessary to bring reforms in individuals but also to re-fashion the enveloping institutions. The institutions are founded on power relations. They give birth to the political order based on power. This is again based on coercive capacity of the state.[76]

Political power enters the scene when the clash of interests surfaces. The clash of interests make the "law" to function as the supreme arbiter. 'State' or the world government functions as arbiter through law. It legitimizes its actions. But, the triumph of law does not always assure the triumph of justice. The claim of law is linked with the facts of power and value. The material inequality constitute the principle basis for order. Then power, and not common standards, becomes the dominant organizing principle of the political system.[77]

It is a common experience that law making and its adjudication favour some over others. When this is realized by deprived groups, cries go up for equalizing condition of life and removing inequalities for justice. If the political order forcefully and effectively responds to these cries, the way is paved for it to assume more and more power, threatening individual liberty. If, on the other hand, it settles on a path of least interference, its legitimacy faces gradual erosion and the prospects of uncertainty and instability look large.[78] Finally, the state assumes absolute power and 'absolute power corrupts absolutely'. Hence, Gandhi suggests decentralization of power within the state. He advocates many power centers within the state.[79] The decentralization of powers undermines the primacy of the state. He, thus, suggests the strategy of decentralization of power upto the village level. He is against concentration of power at the top whatever may be the form of government. The decentralization of power, he believes, breaks down the monopoly structure of power.

According to this new structure, organization of the political system must begin from the bottom and move through intermediate levels to the national level. Since the local community will have the basic responsibility and power to manage its own affairs, the overriding importance that we assign today to the national government will be greatly reduced.[80] Thus, Gandhi wants the problems of the people to be solved by themselves. It can be done by claiming autonomy of an individual which he has surrendered to the state in the course of history. The regaining of autonomy on the part of man will bring back his identity. The preservation of identity non-violently, in a non-violent state, within the disarmed world government, will preserve the ultimate dignity of human being.

Thus, the question of world government to Gandhi, is secondary. He, however, wants it to emerge basically to tone-down the interest based power-politics. The world government, therefore, will have function to coordinate and manage global problems affecting mankind.

Gandhi, thus, wants to create a world order not on coercive power, but on moral forces. Its main organizing principle is not 'power', but 'dignity' of an individual. The world order thus, depends on the extent to which person becomes moral sound and establish relations with external world on the basis of certain ethical standards.

Harmony Between Man and Environment

We have seen how Gandhi removes 'power' from the axis as a main source of conflict by his principle of decentralization of power. The strategy of decentralization breaks down the monopoly of power. Yet the problem remains how to remove conflict of man with nature. In other words how to create harmony between man and his environment.

Man's relations with nature has never been so strained as it is today. Gandhi actually calls it a civilizational crisis. He relates man's greed with the desire to dominate others. Modern civilization places, as Gandhi sees it, the pursuit of self-interest as deemed both natural and rational, restrains imposed on it are considered to be restrictive of the full flowering of the individual self. The pursuit of self-interest pushes out the pursuit of higher values such as spirituality, morality, etc.[81] What is resentful for Gandhi is that violence becomes the dominant characteristic of this civilization. The more regrettable thing to him is that the present civilization does not suggest which appetite has to be satisfied and which to be suppressed, or where to stop. Hence, life becomes a ceaseless struggle for acquiring more and more for oneself.

This would not have become a problem if resources were abundant and every desire could be satisfied without sacrificing others or conflicting with others. Since this is not the case, in to quote Gandhi, 'life corroding competition' starts, which leads us to exploitation, domination, inequality and oppression.[82]

Such a competition for conflicting interests is reflected not only in the relationship of man with man and nature, but also in the relationship of one country with another. This puts an enormous premium on acquisition of resources at the cost of others' welfare.[83] At the world level, state competes with other state for access to and control over resources, located outside its boundaries. It also wants to control and regulate the environmental forces that may impinge on its security and development. Each state is competing with others in the absence of internationally accepted political authority. In such situation, each state has to rely on his self-capacity and physical power. How then, can order be maintained in international society? According to Gandhi, under the circumstances, order can never be maintained. It is a state of affairs free for all and it is heading towards a self-destruction.

We, therefore, need to transcend international order as it is based on 'threat system'. At any moment, the war may break out and the war fought with nuclear armaments is even suicidal. Hence, the necessity of world order has to be based on restriction of human needs and appropriate technology.

Restriction of Human Needs

What should be the purpose of life—is the fundamental question. Gandhi perceives that the purposes of life is to pursue high ideals like truth, Non-violence, justice etc. And the needs of ordinary life - cloth, food, shelter etc. - should be infrastructure to the former. What Gandhi sees, is the fulfillment of needs of ordinary life has remained a sole concern of human existence with higher significance assigned to it. It is considered natural and essential. The main pursuit of man has been to satisfy biological needs and not to bother moral fulfillment of moral self-realization. The central concern of life has become happiness. Happiness through satisfying desires. It now seems possible that these desires can be fulfilled through the transformation and control of nature with the help of technology. Technological innovations increase and proliferate man's needs, which, in turn, stimulates further technological innovations and so on. This requires access to and control over material resources without which needs can not be fulfilled. This situation gives birth to a clash of interests between man and man and between state and state.[84] To this Gandhi suggests a simple solution. Although it sounds simple it is very difficult to put into practice. He says man is a bundle of desires. Gandhi wants that one should ask direct questions to those desire. What is needed and what is wanted? The need based desire should be fulfilled and other desires be given-up. This is a simple way to discriminate what is a good desire and what is a bad one. If one learns to discriminate, the civilizational crisis can be resolved.

Appropriate Technology

Another solution which Gandhi suggests is to apply appropriate technology. Gandhi is not against big machines *per se* but he is against the use of machine to exploit individuals. However, he is against those machines based on complicated and heavy technology which can lead to large scale environmental pollution, ecological decay, resource depletion, impoverishment and exploitation of the masses. He is against the machine culture which creates inequality and restricts employment. He is also against heavy and high speed transport system which came into existence and continues in existence to subserve the vested interests of the imperialist and commercial establishments and military-industrial complexes.[85]

Gandhi although stands for decentralization of production by machine, he is not always against centralized and mass production. He is, however, against the centralized production of the basic necessities of life, like food and clothing. The means of producing them should remain under the control of the people, as air and water are under God's control.[86] But the basic solution he suggests is adoption of appropriate technology. The appropriate technology has many meanings. But it must meet two conditions, i.e., first, it should not render the mass of people unemployed and secondly, it should not poison the eco-system.

Man, Machine and Material have ultimately led to dehumanizing of man. His real-original self, what Rousseau regards as "native man" is lost in a concrete, materialistic mechanically and technologically operated world. It is only through the techniques suggested by Gandhi that man and nature co-exist and one may hope to save the world from great catastrophe.

To sum up, Gandhi agrees with the view that nation-states create order in international society but it is not adequate. It is unjust order and needs to be modified. It does not remove anarchy but adds to it. In order to create an ideal global society, the nation-states are required to be reconstructed and human society must reorganize itself. It can ideally reorganize itself provided its focal point becomes the preservation of human dignity. The preservation of human dignity must be the guiding principle of reorganizing human society. If it is done, the just and peaceful world order can be created. Thus, Gandhi's approach is basically human-centric, neither power-oriented nor institutional oriented. Now, we need to view of Nehru's conception. Although Nehru was Gandhi's disciple, and, like his political guide, dissatisfied with the present order, his conception registers a sharp difference to Gandhi's. He suggests institutional approach to create a just and peaceful world order.

NOTES AND REFERENCES

NOTES ON GANDHI

1. Gandhi had extensively written on the transformation of individual. But this study takes into account of only those views of Gandhi which has international dimension. It seems, Gandhi wanted every individual to be an 'institution' unto himself. If man behaves like an institution, he will learn to rule over himself (swaraj) then no other institution (even nation-state) will be necessary for emancipating thc humankind.
2. R. Chakrabarti, "Gandhian View of the Nation-State as a Constituent of the International Community", in V.T. Patil (ed.) *Study in Gandhi*, Sterling, New Delhi, 1984, pp. 155-62.
3. *Harijan*, December 28, 1938.
4. *Collected Works*, vol. 48, pp. 419-20.
5. *Harijan*, vol. 4, p. 109.
6. M. Gandhi, *Hind Swaraj*, Navjivan, Ahmedabad, 1962, Chapter 16.
7. *Collected Works*, Vol. 15, p. 285. Also see Vol. 38, p. 160.
8. *Collected Work*, Vol. 45, p. 319; and vol., 18, p. 133.
9. *Harijan*, vol. 6, p. 395.
10. Ibid., vol. 48, p. 85.
11. Puri Rashmi Sudha, Praegar, New York, 1987, p. 199.
12. Ibid., p. 219.
13. Ibid., p. 200.
14. *Collected Works*, vol. 31, p. 181.
15. Puri Rashmi Sudha, Op.cit., No. 11.
16. N.G.S. Kini, "Gandhian Contribution to the Theory of Politics", in V.t. Patil (ed.) *Studies in Gandhi*, p. 3016.

17. Ibid.
18. Ibid.
19. Nirmal Kumar Bose, *Studies in Gandhism*, Navjivan, Ahmedabad, 1947, Second Edition, pp. 25-26 and 29.
20. Ibid., p. 26.
21. Paul F. Power, *Gandhi on World Affairs*, George Allen, London, 1960, p. 54.
22. Ibid., p. 67
23. Ibid., p. 67.
24. *Harijan*, vol. 7. pp. 89 and 272; vol. 6, p. 395.
25. Quoted in Puri, Op.cit., No. 11 p. 166.
26. Ibid., p. 166.
27. Pyarelal, Mahatma Gandhi, *The Last Phase*, vol. 1, Navjivan, Ahmedabad, 1956, p. 117.
28. *Collected Works*, vol. 17, p. 435.
29. *Harijan*, vol. 6, p. 282.
30. Quoted in Puri, Op.cit., No. 11, p. 166.
31. *Collected Works*, vol. 28, p. 141.
32. *Harijan*, vol. 7, p. 288.
33. *Harijan*, Garland, New York, vol. 6, p. 282.
34. S.C. Gangal, p. 158.
35. Paul Power, p. 54.
36. Gandhi's views on war were go on changing. For evolution of his views on war, please refer Puri.
37. Quoted in Puri, p. 59. It seems Gandhi's views on war in influenced by his reading and interpreting Mahabharata. As Pandavas were fighting the war for just cause, however, they distasted the war. Gandhi seems to be influenced by Lord Krishna's views on the war, that no one could remain neutral when all out war breaks out in order to preserve some value system which is considered 'just' by one party.
38. Ibid., p. 59.
39. Ibid., p. 59.
40. *Collected Works*, vol. 14, pp. 462-63; and vol. 16, p. 4.
41. Paul Power, p. 60.
42. Ibid., p. 57.
43. Ibid., pp. 63-65.
44. Rameshwar Roy, p. 227.
45. Ibid., p. 227.
46. Paul Power, p. 53.
47. Ibid., p. 53.

48. Theme of 'Hind Swaraj' revolves round to this idea.
49. Rameshwar Roy, p. 231.
50. *Collected Works of Mahtma Gandhi*, Government of India Publication Division, vol. iv, p. 170.
51. Dalla Dhiren Mohan, *The Philosophy of Mahatma Gandhi*, Wisconsin, USA, 1953, pp. 136-37.
52. Nirmal Bore, *Selections From Gandhi*, p. 41.
53. Ibid., p. 113.
54. Pyarelal, *Last Phase*, vol. 1, p. 118.
55. Pyarelal, *Mahatma Gandhi : The Last Phase*, vol. 1, p. 120.
56. Ibid., p. 128.
57. *Harijan*, vol. 9, p. 165.
58. *Collected Works*, vol. 35, p. 457.
59. Ibid., Vol. 15, pp. 104-5.
60. Ibid., vol. 28. p. 441.
61. Ibid., vol. 48, pp. 416-41.
62. S.C. Gangal, "Gandhi and World Order", in K.P. Mishra and S.C. Gangal (ed.), *Gandhi and the Contemporary World, Studies in Peace and War*, Chanakya, Delhi, 1981, pp. 166-67. The entire article is suggested to read on Gandhi's technique of the conflict resolution.
63. Ibid., pp. 166-67.
64. Joan Bonduran, *Conquest of Violence*, Princeton University Press, USA, 1958. See also Arne Naess, "A Systematisation of Gandhian Ethics of Conflict Resolution", *Journal of Conflict Resolution*, vol. 2, June 1958, pp. 1040-55; Ashakant Nimbark, "Gandhism Reexamined", in *Social Research*, New York, vol. 31, March 1964, pp. 94-125.
65. Rameshwar Roy, p. 228.
66. Ibid., p. 231.
67. Ibid.
68. Ibid., p. 228.
69. Ibid., p. 232.
70. Ibid., p. 234.
71. Ibid., p. 232.
72. Ibid., p. 233.
73. *Hind Swaraj*, p. 64.
74. N.K. Bose, *Selections from Gandhi*, p. 254.
75. Ibid., p. 255.
76. Rameshwar Roy, p. 277.
77. Ibid., p. 229.

78. Ibid.
79. V.T. Patil and I.A. Lokapur, "Gandhi's Concept of Decentralisation: Analysis", in V.T. Patil (ed.) p. 109.
80. Rameshwar Roy, p. 234.
81. Ibid., p. 227.
82. Ibid.
83. Ibid.
84. Ibid.
85. S.C. Gangal, Op.cit., No. 62, p. 161.
86. Quoted by S.C. Gangal, Op.cit., No. 62, p. 136, from *Young India*, Vol. III, November 15, 1928, p. 381.

Chapter 3

NEHRU'S CONCEPTION OF INTERNATIONAL SOCIETY

This chapter examines international dimension of Jawaharlal Nehru's views on international society. The four basic theoretical inquiries addressed to his conception are : (a) how does he conceive the international society and how is (dis)order maintained in that society; (b) which strategy he suggests to affect the change in the present (dis)order; (c) how an individual, an important component of international society, has to change himself; and (d) how the mankind has to transform itself to create an international society of mankind to replace the existing society of states.

Nature and Functioning of International Society : The Organizing and Operational Principles of Society

In Nehru's view, international society is primarily composed of the nation-states. He gives secondary importance to the people who reside within the boundaries of the nation-states. The main focus of Nehru's thinking was the operation of the nation-states and their institutions. According to Nehru, the nation-state (system) does not function in isolation. It operates within the global atmosphere. The global atmosphere gives birth to new realities, Nehru called it a new civilization, with which the nation-states are not able cope with. Its response is not adequate enough to meet the challenge of realities. Hence, the objective reality takes over them. The society of nation-states has to take the cognizance of the new forces shaping reality (science, technology, public opinion, internationalism etc.) and needs to accommodate these forces. For Nehru, the basis of nation-states remains nationalism and sovereignty, but their meaning and context has to be changed. Hence, Nehru suggests change in the operational milieu of nation-states, so that they should not become dysfunctional or destroy themselves. We will discuss Nehru's suggestions of operational principles.

According to Nehru, the nation-states have two bases, viz., nationalism and sovereignty. Nationalism and sovereignty are the backbone on which strength of a nation is organized. They gave them (states) status and membership in the comity of nations. They earn them a legitimate membership of the international society. If the international society has to continue its survival, Nehru thinks, the force of nationalism has to develop its international dimension giving up its narrow vision. The attribute of sovereignty, no doubt, helps the nation to preserve its autonomy within the comity of nations. But the time has come to modify its absolute character and a nation has to give up a part of its sovereignty if the international society has to survive and, subsequently, to prosper.

Changing Meaning and Role of Nationalism

Nehru recognizes the role of nationalism in a nation-state system. He agrees that nationalism is a factor binding people of the sovereign states together, from within. It is an emotional force within a domestic society. He considers it virtuous too. Nehru attributes certain virtues in nationalism as it contributes "vigour, growth, unity, self esteem to those who ever cared to be guided by it".[1]

For Nehru, nationalism is a good servant and a bad master. On elaborating the strength and weakness of the force of nationalism, Nehru states, "Nationalism, of course, is a curious phenomenon which at a certain stage, in a country's history, gives life, growth, strength and unity; but, at the same time, it has tendency to limit because one thinks of one's country as something different from the rest of the world... The result is that the same nationalism which is the symbol of growth for a people becomes a symbol of the cessation of that growth in the mind. Nationalism, when it becomes successful, sometimes goes on spreading in an aggressive way and becomes a danger internationally".[2]

Thus, Nehru recognizes the inherent strength and weaknesses of the force of nationalism and advocates some sort of balance between the two inherent tendencies of nationalism. He cautions that if some measures are not taken the goodness of it (force of nationalism) will turn into evil. He wrote, "...some kind of balance must be found. Otherwise, something that was good can turn into evil".[3]

While comparing nationalism with internationalism, Nehru agrees with those who believe that internationalism is a thing of future, and nationalism must fade away. What worries Nehru is that, whenever a country or the world faces a crisis (war) nationalism becomes immediately dominant. At the time of war, people turn to nationalism immediately. Every country that was involved in the Second World War became tremendously nationalistic. Nationalist framework did provide sense of security to states but in the process each nation was seeking security under its own umbrella. This individualist notion of nationalism divided states and internationalism could never become a genuine concern and force or states.

Nehru visualizes two tendencies namely nationalism and internationalism. According to him both these develop simultaneously in the international society. Nehru sees internationalism in the activities of proletarian elements of the world. It develops perhaps more significantly in the realm of finance, trade, and commerce. Nehru recognizes the growth of internationalism in the development of science, new commerce, the radio and cinema etc.

Hence, for, Nehru the problem is how to reconcile these two conflicting conceptions—nationalism and internationalism. Nehru wrote, "Nationalism obviously is something deep down in human nature. We can not uproot it and there is no reason why we should try to uproot it, because, nationalism ultimately depends on all that is best in us".[4] Speaking on another occasion he once said, "On the other hand internationalism is not only good but essential in the world today. And yet some kind of vague internationalism without definite contacts and bonds with nationalism is almost an airy nothing. How to combine the two?"[5]

It seems Nehru eventually arrives at a conclusion that, internationalism as evolving with the passage of time has yet to acquire a concrete shape. While nationalism is a concrete thing. It is binding people and giving them identity. Since nationalism is an integral part of the people—who have already achieved nationhood—it is to stay side by side with a modern state.

Nehru suggests ways and means to combine the two. He suggests that it should be freed from imperialism and racialism and made subject to rationalism. If this is done nationalism can become a building block of a future peaceful global order and a stable international society can be created out of it.

In Nehru's view, the nationalism is mixed with imperialism and racialism. It teaches exploitation of the powerless by powerful nations. To Nehru, a true international order can emerge provided the exploitation of the weak and the powerless by the powerful comes to end. He firmly believes that the problem of racialism is mixed with nationalism. This problem, therefore, needs to be solved urgently. It should be solved in such a way that it leaves no hatred behind which can embitters relations between nations.

Even if nationalism is freed from imperialism as well as from racialism, Nehru still holds it to be narrow, unless it is subject to rationalism. In order to evolve a rational nationalism, one must keep one thing in mind that nations and their nationalism are not ends in themselves. He wants nations to grow out of their narrow grooves of thought and action, and pay attention to the synthesis between national interest and international interest. Being a pragmatic idealist, he does not mind giving primacy to the national interest by keeping in mind the interdependence of states and remembering that the welfare of one's own state is intertwined with the welfare of the whole world community.[6] According to him this is not narrowness. He thus, advocates a balance between nationalism and internationalism. The primacy of national interest is the rule for Nehru but also he wants that it must be synchronized with the international interest. This requires promoting maximum cooperation between nations. The nation-state should not operate only on the basis of nationalism if it wants to survive, but at the same time each nation has to take into account the interests of the other nations as well. The nation-states unite the people living within their territory in terms of the similarities of their problems and aspirations.

Nehru firmly believes that nationalism, devoid of internationalism, would not serve the purpose. Now the time has come, due to the development of science and technology, that either nations can survive or perish jointly in the atomic age. Secondly, nation-stated have become interdependent economically and otherwise. Hence, whatever problems were considered as national yesterday have become global problems today.

Nehru discards modern realism based on the ideas of Machiavelli[7] (and Hobbes). Nehru believes that Machiavelli taught us to look upon 'state' as a separate thing" as if it is distinctly a separate part of the society of nations. He does not teach us to look at one's national interest in terms of the larger good of the world.

All the major problems which man faces today are global problems. Even local problems are now tied up with "dozens and dozens of other questions that agitate the world. For him, there is nothing like Indian, Asian, European problems. Virtually all problems are global and they can be solved only on a world scale. Hence, Nehru advocates the teaching of 'world history' to the students in the school and colleges along with the history of an individual's country. The history of one country can not be understood without examining it in the international context,[8] a view Nehru holds. Identity of the people does matter in the creation of the nation-state, but having served its purpose (sense of physical and emotional belonging), in order to keep pace with the changing time, it is essential to have a much wider perspective of the nation-a perspective which can accommodate others.

Competition

Being the Prime Minister as well as the Foreign Minister of India, at one time, Nehru was operating India's foreign policy within the international system. But he was not satisfied the way the sovereign states were operating. According to him it would breed violence and war. It would vulgarize people all over the world. The nation-state system he opines, makes nations brutal in thought, speech and action. It encourages competition instead of co-operation among them. Nehru thinks that an old order based on competition, needs to be replaced by a new order based on co-operation. He does not advocate co-operation of two or more powerful nations for exploitation, or some regional co-operation. If it happens, Nehru believes it will result in the struggle for power, and the world will be worse off than it was before. He firmly maintains that the basic need is global cooperation, and the idea of one world should be kept paramount.[9] For nations, it is imperative to learn to tolerate, and to peacefully coexist resulting in the extension of the idea of national into international relations. "It means an attitude of live and let live and a belief in the power of example and persuasion rather than in arbitrament by force".[10] This quotation of Nehru clarifies that he clearly distinguishes national life (society) from international society. He advocates that as communities tolerate each other within the nation, the nation must learn to tolerate each other (as individual state) within global society so that the peaceful coexistence between the nations can be ensured. The nation-state has only to emulate their own example.

Nehru argues that if we look at the problems in the global context, there was no real conflict between the basic national interests of states. But, they give priorities to their problems differently. Hence, their perceptions of national interests differ. This varied scheme of priorities make it hard for states to co-operate smoothly. The great need, therefore, today is that nation-state system should work with the United Nations for some meaningful form of cooperation.

In the economic sphere too, Nehru argues underdeveloped nations of the third world were dragged on to the path of progress. They must be helped to rise. Only by helping them to rise, all humanity would rise with them. Nehru believes that if one part of the world goes down economically, the entire world will be affected adversely by it. Hence, rich nations should help the poor, not out of generosity, but out of enlightened self-interest.[11]

In Nehru's view, international cooperation means international tolerance. We are today, by and large, sufficiently civilized in the context of our national communities to tolerate and regard others as the bases of communal life within our national societies. Without it, national groups and, certainly democratic institutions, can not survive.

Nehru does not question the rationale of the emergence of the nation-states system. He does not even object to its not being dynamic with the changing time and circumstances. It was status-quoist. Those states which have the privilege of being a part of the Westphalia system have adopted somewhat a fragmented view of the world. The European states have the advantage of at least 300 years in terms of their sovereign independent statehood. They have been perpetuating economic imperialism by greater co-operation among themselves. This has produced greater co-operation within the area of autarchy, but autarchy has ultimately created isolation from the rest of the world. Nehru says, "I do not believe in a narrow autarchy. But the internationalism that I look forward to is not one of common subjection, imposed from above but a union and a co-operation of free nations for the common good. It is this kind of world order that will bring peace and progress to mankind.[12]

As we saw earlier, Nehru stands for nation-state system (and its continuation) but, his main thrust is to improve the status-quoist system. The Westphalian system has been confined to only Western Europe. In other words, Nehru once demanded the imperialist powers to free Afro-Asian nations and to assign them a status of sovereign independent nations. He advocates the expansion of nation-state system throughout the globe. Nehru's main objective in advocating freedom for every country including India was, in the words of Professor A.P. Rana, "the extension of the Western Westphalia to the rest of the world".[13] The Western Westphalia freed the Western European states from the Roman Empire as well as from the overlordship of the Church authority in seventeenth century. In the same way, Nehru wanted that the Western Powers should free all the nations of Asia and Africa from its subjugation.

While referring to this demand of Nehru, Professor A.P. Rana, calls it "Eastern Westphalia". Thus, Nehru pleaded for the universalization of the international society. The central point in the formation of the present modern state system is the liberation of states. States which were under some form of subjugation. Eastern Westphalia will complete the Circle releasing remaining states from subjugation.

Before 1950s, Nehru was advocating the universalization of international society and after 1950s, he was advocating democratization of the international society. The decolonization process which started in the late forties and fifties, had given birth to many small sovereign states. But they were not treated equally. They were not given chance to participate in the decision-making process at the global level. He was committed to the democratization of international society. It was evident in his opposition to any kind of hegemonic inter-nationalism. Nehru believed that if they were not granted an equal status in the comity of nations, he wrote, "small states in the world of tomorrow have no future in store and they are sure to be reduced to the satellite states..."[14] Having this conviction in mind, he advocated a free and equal status of every nations, small or big in the international institutions like the United Nations Organization (UNO) or the British Commonwealth. Unless it is done, in Nehru's view, no durable international order can be created.

Power Politics

Nehru knew that the main driving force of the three hundred year old sovereign state system was power-politics. He was also aware of the changing nature of power-politics. He, therefore, advocated a different sort of game of power politics mainly based on diplomacy. With the advent of the weapon system of mass destruction and the enlightened public opinion demanding higher standard of living, as Nehru believes, these new forces have created new demand on the nation-states system.

According to Nehru, after the Second World War, the international relations no longer remained the old game of chess. It was no longer a game in which nations could come together for some territorial possession or some other gain. Many new factors and actors emerged on the world stage that made relations among state something quite different from what they had been. It accentuated the need for a quite different inter-state system. The new factor of public opinion on a mass scale demanded a higher standard of living and better condition for the people from the government of a country. The foreign policies of the governments today, therefore, are being determined by this demand everywhere.[15]

While commenting on the likely impact of the atomic weapons on international relations. Nehru said that the new weapon system had changed the character of the game of power politics. The notion of 'power for power's sake' has become out of date. The nuclear weapons changed the tone and the texture of international politics. hence, according to Nehru, the need of hour was a new international order. He advocated a new order which could accommodate the twin desires of the masses : not to have large scale suicidal war; and desire for a higher standard of living.

Nehru looks at the game of power politics as an ephemeral historical accident and that it can be totally abolished. He firmly believes that power politics can be moderated, the degree of hostility can be decreased, the diplomacy of accommodation can be practiced within the general framework of power. He declares faith in man. Man's attitudes, institutions and methods can be improved even if they can not be perfected. It needs to be borne in mind that Nehruvian approach does not in reality forbid the use of power politics so long as man's attitude, institutions and methods do not change. Nehru, however, "forbids the use of only those types of power that involve physical violence and that are unworkable without an atmosphere of hostility. All other types of power-economic, psychological, and moral—are permissible provided they are used according to certain guiding principles such as honesty, truth and so on".[16] Nehru, thus, does not believe that power politics is inherent in the nature of organized society, hence, (in Nehru's view) it can be modified and ultimately abolished.

Nehru does not make any suggestion as to how power of non-violence can be applied in international relations, although, he had seen its meaningful application in the national struggle. He is, however in favour of economic sanction to check aggressor states. And he is also in favour of applying the force of world public opinion. He does not have objection to the technique of foreign aid and the dissemination of information to foreign peoples, provided certain rules are followed.[17]

Nehruvian approach of power politics means abandoning military alliance and military power in the interest of the world. However, he is in favour of keeping it intact for the use in emergency. No nation can banish it, as is a usual custom to support her foreign policy. Simultaneously, a nation has to abandon the age old practice of keeping her own people united and loyal to it by inappropriate campaign of portraying foreign states as enemies and spreading hatred against them.

Now the problem arises: if military power is permitted to be used in emergency, how much of it a nation can keep? Nehru seems to have the following answer: (i) nation needs power enough to defeat the attacker, cost of attack should be so high and its reward so low that the attack will not be worth; (ii) the weakening of a state's military power might be offset automatically by the strengthening of some other forms of power, i.e., its moral and psychological influence will increase. It is also possible that transferring money from military programme to economic and social betterment might increase her economic and social influence. In propounding this thesis, Nehru seems to presume that "much of the military power now existing has proved to be useless in many situations because no one dares using it.[18]

To sum up, Nehru does not advocate power-politics backed by weapons. To him, the days of military power are over as the atomic weapons can't be used. Hence, he advocates non-military power, that is, economic power. The power of purse will bring social improvement (internally) as well as political influence vis-a-vis other nations.

Being a professional politician and a seasoned statesman, Nehru knew that, the road to war goes through conflicting perceptions which is unavoidable. According to him, if perception is corrected, conflicts can also be resolved to everyone's advantage. Nehru thinks there are really no basis for conflicts among either individuals or states. What he pleads is a dialogue between the parties in dispute in a climate of mutual good will and benefit. The Stoic school of thought has always believed that if all individuals and states could discover their real interests, they would all live in harmony. Nehru pleads that this should be one of the organizing principles of international order.

Nehru seems to condemn the methods which are used in the existing international order. They are the methods of violence, force, crusading, organizing alliances and counter-alliances etc. All these methods are implied in the term power-politics. Nehru outrightly rejects that form of power-politics of the existing international order.

Nehru has formed, what A.P. Rana calls, "a menacing view to power politics and the balance of power".[19] Nehru thinks that the theory of balance of power inevitably leads to conflict and war.[20]

Nehru rejects the concept of foreign policy based on the traditional concept of power-politics. In his opinion, the present reality of international politics, does not take us anywhere. On the countrary, it works against the true national interests in the long run. This type of reality degrades morality and justice to the secondary consideration. In the context of a new civilization, the major objective of foreign policy should not be only power. It must promote values like justice, fairness and tolerance. The power (political) approach, in Nehru's views, put the aspirations, idealism and morality of the masses in the background.[21]

Nation-States and Ideologies

Nehru views, the current nation-state system, which is based on the principles of competition, conflict and exploitation, is further buttressed by the different political ideologies which they prescribe not only for themselves but for other nations too. A nation adopts a particular ideology, viz. Fascism, Nazism, Capitalism, or Communism, for their emancipation. But it also wants to impose its Ideology on other nation-state. Ideologies have become a tool in the hands of nation-states for the game of power-politics. It divides nations and never creates a climate of co-operation among them. It should be noted that Nehru did not blame people for adopting those ideologies. He blames different conflicting systems which different ideologies create in international relations as none of the existing ideologies, was Capitalism, Fascism (Nazism) or Communism can unite the nation-states. They do not respond to the new realities. He, therefore, advocates an ideology of democratic socialism which can address the new politico-economic reality and help to create a new and stable world order. Let us examine Nehru's views on different ideologies one by one. Any ideology which dehumanizes man and his fellow human beings as mere means to ends may not survive long. Such ideologies have seeds of their own destruction. Nehru's apprehension were vindicated when Nazism and Fascism collapsed. Probably, communism might have to meet the same fate.

The Germans, Japanese and Italians were living under the Fascist system which impelled them to behave as they did. According to Nehru, it is a system which denies freedom and is based on violence and aggression. Nehru, therefore, refuses to condemn individual German or Japanese, for the horrors the systems and caused in the world. To him, whether an individual, German or Japanese is good or bad is irrelevant, for 'evil lies in the system'. Nehru does not have faith in Fascism as a system as it has no intention to solve the global problems of exploitation, poverty and misery. On the contrary, it adds to the problems.

Nehru keeps a soft corner for Marxism and appreciates the Russian experiment with Marxism. One aspect of Marxism which impressed him is its historical interpretation of the forces of the world history.

Economic System

Nehru held the view that it was capitalism which was largely responsible for the excessive nationalism in the late nineteenth and early twentieth centuries. The capitalistic system is responsible also for modern imperialism as it divides nations. Modern technological development can evolve a global economy which would cater to the needs of the mankind properly. But the modern capitalism comes in the way and does not allow the emergence of global economic system based on justice. It happens because, the vested interests that controlled the governments of various capitalist nations rejected the idea of internationalism. On the contrary, they have promoted economic nationalism, hence, industrialized nations have become more intense rivals than ever before. According to Nehru, the capitalist system has shown no capacity to adjust to the new era of science. Nehru, therefore, wants capitalism to make way in favour of socialism which stands at the threshold carrying idea of international economic co-operation.[22] The contention is that, capitalism did not modify itself according to the growing impact of science. Similarly, Communism did not adopt itself to the growing demands of consumerism which rest on market, competition, investment and lack of state control. It is in this context that one may agree that Nehru looked for middle path of socialism whether the best of both the systems, (Capitalism and Communism) may be incorporated (Private and Public Sectors).

Nehru fully agrees with Marx's perception of history as a struggle between the few who own the means of production and the large masses of who own nothing. He never accepts Marx uncritically. He finally comes to the conclusion that Marxism might have done some good to the Russian society in defeating the old forces of feudalism, imperialism and colonialism, but Marxism as a comprehensive and systematic philosophy of society is 'out of date'.

Nehru has special attraction for democratic system and, hence, advocated democracy for independent India. But he was disillusioned with the Western democracies when they started appeasing the fascist forces. He feared that the communist forces will win, will take over and dominate the world. Nehru was further disappointed when the democracies showed no sign of fighting for a new order. Those like England, France etc., rather, fought to maintain the old worn-out order of the past— feudalism, colonialism, etc.

A year after the end of the Second World War, Nehru reiterated his charge that the allies had not fought the war to produce a new civilization. The Western democracies just expressed lip sympathy to democracy, freedom and peace as they refused to accelerate the process of decolonization.

With the advent of the Cold War (1950s), Nehru was disillusioned with democracy in England, France and the USA, when he saw that the wartime allies were again preparing for a new war instead of a new world order. To him, it was a further evidence that the people of the world were betrayed.[23] The Allied powers stood and fought in the name of democracy against fascism. But on winning the war, they were reluctant to give up their colonies. They had procured the support of the colonized people during the war. They had told them that they were fighting for the survival of democracy. They had also assured them that they would be granted freedom, if they would win. Nehru felt betrayed when he saw no chance of assurances coming true.

Economic System

In 1930s, the laissez-faire type of capitalism was prevalent. Nehru thought that, this type of capitalism would disappear. This old type of capitalism, to him, was "a kind of luxury system for well-to-do nations". According to him, the laissez-faire type of capitalism proved that it had its own limitations and disabilities. It failed to cope with the challenge of the great depression of 1930s. The days of capitalism were over and whatever remnant of it were left, require to be modified by greater planning and control as the Russian had done it successfully.

Nehru, therefore, convincingly, advocates the replacement of capitalism by socialism. To him, socialism is more than an economic doctrine. It was a philosophy of life. He writes, "I see no way of ending the poverty, the vast unemployment, the degradation and the subjection of the Indian people except through socialism. That involves vast and revolutionary changes in our political and social structure, the ending of vested interests in land and industry, as well as the feudal autocratic Indian states system. That means the ending of private property, except in a restricted sense, and the replacement of the present profit system by a higher ideal of cooperative service. It means ultimately a change in our instincts and habits and desires. In short, it means a new civilization, radically different from the present capitalist order.[24]

The quotation clearly indicates Nehru's strong conviction in favour of socialism which is beyond the tenets of mere economic salvation — it could usher in a new civilization in the world.

While addressing the All India Congress Committee on 4th January 1957, he defined the democratic socialism as follows :

1. The substitution of co-operation in place of acquisitiveness;
2. Equal opportunity for development of personality to every one; and
3. The democratic process of peaceful and legitimate methods to achieve these two goals.[25]

In short, to Nehru, socialism with human face was more acceptable rather than under the cover of more authoritarian governance. The new civilization was required to discard old systems and to create a new political, economic and social systems based on equality, progress, science, co-operation and freedom.

Nehru on War

Nehru ascribes different causes to different types of war. But basically, he believes that the root cause of any war is psychological in nature. Nations, like individuals, fear each other, and live in constant insecurity. The most fundamental cause of war, to Nehru, is not lust for power, greed etc., but 'fear' of each other. It breeds war within the international society. Secondly, Nehru believes that the wars break out because existing institutions fail to cope with the new reality or situation. The people demand a new order based on justice, and the nation-states fail to respond to it. This results into a warfare. The cause of war, therefore, keep changing according to the period of history. Once upon a time in history, religion and kings were generating order in society, but when they lost their hold, wars were fought in the name of religion. In some period, wars were essentially religious or dynastic in nature.

In Nehru's view, in his time wars were essentially economic or political in nature. The old order was based on imperialism, colonialism, racialism and capitalism; hence, it was responsible for the outbreak of wars, especially the first world war.[26]

Nehru compares capitalism with modern imperialism and holds it chiefly responsible for the modern war. By narrating the history of imperialism, Nehru ascertains how and why modern imperialism caused wars. In his letters (1933) to his daughter, Indira (1933), he describes three kinds of imperialism : crude, subtle and perfect. In a crude form of imperialism, the victorious powers annex both the conquered land and its peoples, making them slaves. In a subtle form, the imperialists annex only the conquered land but the people are not enslaved. In this form, people are exploited by various strategies like taxation, trade controls etc. Britishers applied such exploitative strategies in India before the First World War. The third type of imperialism, according to Nehru, is the perfect one as it is invisible by its very nature. It is noticed slowly by people and, hence, there resentment starts against a foreign power slowly. This is a sheer economic imperialism popularly known as capitalism. In this form of capitalism, the dominant country (viz. USA in Latin America) is interested only in economic sphere, i.e., only in profit. They are interested only in controlling the economy of a nation. Nehru firmly maintains that whatever might be the form of imperialism, the common characteristic is exploitation of one group of people by the others.[27]

Imperialism gave birth to two historical situations; the colonies of the imperialists power remained backward and exploited. This made people conscious against the dominant imperialists powers. They got united under the force of nationalism to throw away imperialists power. The underdeveloped and backward people started challenging the basis of old order and demanded a new political and economic order based on justice. This situation disturbed the old 'peaceful equilibrium' and gave birth to an explosive situation. Secondly, other independent countries like, Germany, Italy and Japan united under the fascist forces and started challenging the imperialist powers like, the UK, France, and the USA. The Fascists started challenging them by military means and thus, the seeds of the Second World War were sown. Nehru blamed England and France for not heeding the advice of the President Wilson for the creation of a just world order based on decolonization, universal democracy, total disarmament and the collective security system. But they (England and France) refused and ignored the advice of Wilson. Hence, the old order continued.

Nehru on Peace Treaties

The Treaty of Versailles, according to Nehru, preserved the old order and gave extension of life to that outdated order. Referring to Versailles Treaty, he writes, "We have lived in this era of Versailles Treaty, these twenty years and each succeeding your has brought war and revolution, horror and misery to the people of the world. And yet the old guard politicians who had brought the war and made this peace continued in command and stuck complacently to their old ways which had so often brought disaster..."[28] The dominating fact in the world today is the break-up of the old order, both political and economic, and these broken eggs can not be put together again. The British Empire, represen-ting this dying order, will pass away, and the present economic system will give place to another".[29] The rise of Mussolini in Italy and

Hitler in Germany, was the result according to Nehru, of the British refusal to accept the forces of change which would usher in a new equitable world order. Preservation of the status-quo and refusal to satisfy the aspirations of Fascism — these two finally led the world to conflict. Even after the Second World War, to Nehru's disappointment, the trend remained the same. Nehru reiterated that, the allies had fought the (second) war not to produce a new civilization. The Western democracies just expressed lip sympathy to democracy, freedom the peace.

With the advent of the Cold War, Nehru got disillusioned with democracy when he saw that the wartime allies were again preparing for a new war instead of trying for a new world order.[30] The dominant theme of the cold war was militarism. Nehru's apprehension was that the Cold War would perpetuate the cycle of exploitation in yet another form - neo-colonialism. The emerging Third World countries would be subjugated under the dominance of the developed countries for reason of economic assistance and other help. They (the Third World) also had the legacy of conflicts which would further provide an opportunity to the USA and other western powers to divide them and supply them with weapons and, in turn, seek their dependence. These relations would be motivated purely by economic and military considerations. The developed world would take the advantage of resources, which the Third World could not exploit due to lack of technology and expertise. Such dependence would facilitate the military needs of the cold warriors at the cost of the Third World.

With the end of colonialism and racialism, Nehru perceives, raising of the living standards of people in underdeveloped countries and the promotion of the temper of peace in as wide an area as possible which will help to tackle the roots of conflict.

Nehru is convinced that colonialism and imperialism were the stumbling blocks to world peace. The great powers have a tendency to influence, coerce and dominate the small powers. To Nehru, imperialism was a phase of capitalism. He argues that, imperialism has an inherent characteristic of capitalism. Nehru derives lessons from history that, imperialism breeds unhealthy competition which results in war among the powers.[31] Peace "can only come when the causes of war are removed. So long as there is the domination of one country over another, or the exploitation of one class by another, there will always be attempts to subvert the existing order and no stable equilibrium can endure. Out of imperialism and capitalism peace can never come".[32] To Nehru, a true international order can emerge provided the exploitation of the weak and the powerless by the powerful comes to an end. The abject poverty and untold misery of humankind must be abolished. There can never be stability and peace so long as the vast majority of the human race do not secure freedom from want.

Nehru thinks that it is not only economic exploitation but economic backwardness which undermines the cause of peace.

Racialism

Racialism is a threat to world peace. Nehru believes in the dignity of man and equality of all human beings, irrespective of their racial origin. According to him, racial discrimination is bound to lead to strife and conflicts because, it continues to challenge the self-respect of a vast number of people in the world. Peace in the world can not be maintained, if the bulk of humanity in the third world is enslaved and oppressed.

Nehru firmly believes that, if the problem of racial discrimination is not solved in time, it will lead to disasters of the first magnitude as the problem of racialism is mixed with nationalism. This problem, therefore, needs to be solved urgently. It should be solved in such a way that it would leave hatred behind which may embitter relations between the nations. Appealing on humanitarian ground Nehru writes, "We have to recognize, of course, that, there are countries in this world which are highly developed in many ways, others less developed. They are not all the same, but all of them are human beings, trying to live with dignity of man not putting up with anything else. That is certain".[33]

For Nehru the dignity of human being is the basic thing. If it is not preserved, peace can never be maintained. The abolition of the racial discrimination will be a step in the direction of evolving a peaceful order.

Individual : Another Component of International Society

Primarily, the nation-state system occupies the mind of Nehru and he wants to reach to the people through the nation-states. But he does not neglect the role an individual can play in bringing about a new global order. The nation-state system and the individual are parts of the atmosphere composed of psychological social, political and economic forces. They, unknowingly, interact with these forces. These forces are given birth by, what Nehru calls, the new civilization.[34] The new civilization is based on the forces of science, technology and rationalism.

They have changed the contexts of human life on the earth. According to Nehru, the new civilization has the potential to solve the age-old problems of poverty, ignorance, and exploitation. With the help of technology and science, everyone on the earth could be fed and granted a decent way of living. It is capable of producing a different kind of world — a new civilization. In order to create a new world order, the forces of new civilization need to be understood and utilized for the welfare of the mankind. In order to create a new world order, in Nehru's view, the individual needs to be changed. The individual has to understand the forces of science and technology, and accordingly, he has to change his attitude as well as his behaviour.[35]

Nehru has a pessimistic view of human nature. However, his pessimism is not like that of Hobbes. He grants that man is basically passive but he is capable of change, if he so decides. According to him, man by birth is not good or bad. He is born with a neutral nature. His attitudes and behaviour are later on conditioned and determined by the cultural environment within which he is born and reared.[36] He, therefore stands for change in environmental milieu along with individual. He wants that the two processes should go together. In a letter to his daughter, Indira Gandhi, (1933), he writes about human nature, "man, in spite of his great and vaunted progress, is still very unpleasant and selfish animal".[37]

Nehru desires to create a "new man" which should be rationale, fearless, and have tolerance. If he becomes like that, he will automatically be co-operative and self-disciplined.

Rationalism

Rationalism of Nehru is directly connected with the spirit of scientific inquiry. He does not want people to rely on the authority and faith of religion, which have enchained their minds in superstitution, myth, magic and dogmas. He once told Michael Breacher that, "no country or people who are slave to dogma",[38] can progress. Since it is never dogmatized, it does not require acceptance, or faith, or obedience to authority. Science calls for doubting, questioning, and rational inquiry. Science has respect for the human mind and is tolerant of varying opinions.[39]

Nehru does not want mere application of science in the name of scientist and rationalist. He wants the acceptance of scientific approach as a way of life. He wanted the new civilization composed of men who are critical in their thinking. The scientific man will refuse to accept things without testing, without trial; he must as well as be in an everlasting search for new knowledge. To him, mere agreement without critical thinking is meaningless.

Yet, Nehru cautions that, by merely adopting scientific approach, man will not be able to solve all his problems. He, therefore, wants a science to be allied with philosophy.[40] He advocates democracy and discards authoritarianism because, democracy is based on rationalism while authoritarianism was based on dogma. Democratic search for truth is the very thing that authoritarianism forbids. Secondly, the individual freedom is ensured and encouraged by rationalism and scientism. He loves a world based on reason and science as he thinks that only through these approaches, the problems of misery and ignorance of the masses on be solved.

Fear

According to Nehru the major obstacle to a rational civilization and a rational system of world order is great psychological fixation of fear. It is fear, that is the most basic threat to the survival of the modern world. Fear perverts the behaviour of both individuals and nations. Nations fear nations. The rich fear the poor and blocs of states fear other blocs. The East fears the West and West fears the East. The entire atmosphere of the world is soaked in fear. Fear forbids the use of logic. It reverts men into barbarism, forgetting all civilization they have learned. Fear is the cause of greater tragedies. It is also the cause of more intense fear. the NATO has been created and Germany has been re-armed by the West because of the fear of communism taking over the world.

Nehru argues that man's primary difficulty is psychological. The root cause of many difficulties in society is rooted deep in human psyche which is obsessed with fear complex. The first step to be taken to resolve conflict is to change that attitude. The fear complex exists primarily because, men attempt to achieve their goals by wrong means. They literally frighten their fellow men. The global climate of fear evident in the world is man-made. If it can be removed, the world order based on justice and non-violence can be restored.

Tolerance

The second virtue, which Nehru wants people to imbibed with, is the habit of tolerance. People should be tolerant of each others' idea, ideologies, ways of life, religions and so on. The best life is a life surrounded by a veritable kaleidoscope of behaviour, institutions, systems, ideologies, and practices.

A major cause of intolerance, to Nehru is that, people too often confuse the superficial differences among people with basic differences. The differences in ways of eating, drinking and dressing are a superficial differences and not the basic in nature. In fact, most men are similar in their basic characteristics, that they have more or less the same urges, the same desires, and everyone, except few, wants peace in the world. They not want trouble. They want to live this peaceful domestic life. Thus, basic urges and thoughts of all more or less alike.

The superficial differences produce the terrible fear of one people for another. They fear the unknown and they misunderstand them. This repeatedly produces conflicts. Nehru thinks that the differences were essential for a satisfactory world society. Diversity is a good teacher, he argues. By tolerating differences in states and people, men learn much from each other, even from those with whom they disagree; and that contributes to the progress of all society.

Tolerance is essential for peace. Nehru says, if we really want to avoid war, we have to learn to tolerate much that we do not like and refrain from interfering in each others' affairs. Otherwise, peace is impossible.[41] According to Nehru, tolerant people are not aggressive and nor do they try to impose their views or way of life on other people or nations.

To Nehru, tolerance is not a limitless virtue. Sometimes, there emerges in international society an ideology, a government, or a situation that can not be tolerated. A case in point is Fascism based on aggression and violence. It can not be tolerated by the community of nations. It is dangerous for other nation's survival. In that case, intervention is justified.

This is an exception. In Nehru's design of world order, tolerance is the highest virtue for every individual, community, group or a nation.

Nehru's Strategy for 'Change'

Nehru advocates and tries personally to bring about changes in the nation-state system as well as in the individual. Hence, we need to look at Nehru's philosophy of change one by one, in the following pages.

Nation-State System

Nehru does not favour doing away with the nation-state system *per se*. He wants to maintain the nation-state system, but he is not in favour of the way in which the system is operating. He, therefore, suggests new ways and means for its operation as well as he seeks to bring about changes in the environment within which it is operating. Accordingly he suggested that the nation-state system can not function in isolation. The system operates through the environment. Now the issue is what to change? The nation-states system or the environment in which it has to operate? Nehru provides a clear answer. He favours the change in both — environment and in the nation state system. The nation-state system has its origin in history. It is almost three hundred years old. So far, it has shown resilience and not yet outgrown its utility. It is functional, hence it can not be uprooted overnight. But, Nehru thinks its operational milieu could be changed; hence, he suggests changes in psychological atmosphere from that permeated by hostility, suspicion, and fear to that permeated by rationalism, tolerance, friendship and cooperation. He also suggests to change the political, economic and social environment within which the state-centric system has to operate.

Panchsheel : A Code of Conduct for Nation-State System

With the advent of the Westphalian system of nation-state, some 'rules of the game' emerged for the maintenance of international order. By these rules, the nation-state had to regulate their conduct. These type of regulatory principles include general norm of behaviour. These rules evolved as a result of formal and informal understanding, and are treated in the 'spirit' of agreements, different kind of tacit understanding. Their shared feature is that, they guide the conduct of states in their relations to each other. They also help to prevent conflict and facilitate co-operation. From 1648 to 1945, these normative principles functioned, evolved, decayed, maintained and communicated until the advent of the age of balance of terror.

In the age of nuclear terror, particularly during the period of the Cold War, Nehru thought that, a new code of conduct was necessary to evolve. Hence, he converted the ethical principles-Panchsheel of Lord Buddha into the political principles in order to conduct the game of power-politics in international field in later half of this century.

Panchsheel of Nehru provides a common framework within which the modern sovereign nation-state system with a nuclear teeth can conduct their relations, so that the most feared nuclear war can be averted. They are :

1. mutual respect for each other's territorial integrity and sovereignty;
2. mutual non-aggression;
3. mutual non-interference in each other's internal affairs;

4. equality and mutual benefit; and
5. peaceful coexistence.[42]

These principles of 'Panchsheel' are promising good conduct in the interest of progress, prosperity and peace to the nations of the world. Nehru opines that if these principles are accepted, they will wipe out hatred, distrust, insecurity and mutual antagonism from the body politic of international relations. In fact, Panchsheel is a code of conduct for the nations of the world in order to 'live and let live' in this most dangerous world.

Panchsheel subscribes good conduct on the part of the participators in the game of politics. Needless to say, good conduct is essential for one's amicable and friendly relationship with other nations. These principles will remove fear while conducting relations, will keep violence at bay and will promise that sovereignty of each nation will remain intact. Panchsheel is free from the dogma and other ideologies and preserve freedom for those who uphold them. In the background of the Cold War fought intensely, Nehru offered tolerance, co-operation and respect for each other's way of life, views, and outlooks. Nehru's was a non-dogmatic approach to world peace. Panchsheel advocates a positive philosophy of peace.

World Federation Through the United Nations Organization (UNO)

Nehru always thought that, the world government would be the ideal institution to maintain peace. However distant an ideal it may be, it would be useful to keep this ideal in mind while working, and modifying existing social and political institutions.[43]

He, therefore, suggests to turn the UNO into a world government, as it is better placed and better organized than the League of Nations. Unlike the League, the UNO has universal representation.[44] To Nehru, what is necessary to change is not the system of Veto powers and other procedures of the UNO, but the world as a whole must change. This means all the nations must change and people all over the world must change. We must change the attitude that 'today is the same as yesterday and tomorrow will not differ greatly'. Nations like individuals, must learn to think of their freedom and independence in terms of the world and global co-operation because "the days of isolated national existence are past beyond recall".[45]

Nehru hoped that the UNO could bring all nations together to serve as a commonwealth of nations, where every member state would give up that part of freedom which is necessary for international cooperation.

Nehru wants the UN to serve as an 'umpire' to check the misbehaviour or interference with other countries. He resisted all attempts to reduce the world body into a forum to serve the interests of the power blocs. The world was so divided by divided by different ideologies and military blocs that, he hoped the UNO could make cooperation possible. Such cooperation among countries with "divergent political and economic systems is possible in the world body as long as each country is free to carry on the policy it chooses for itself".[46] Thus, he wants nations to preserve their sovereignty and seek cooperation through sovereign equality of nations, and never at its cost.

The UN in Nehru's view, must be transformed into a world government. It "should be encouraged and supported in every way and should be allowed to develop into some kind of world government or world order".[47] The ideal of "the one world" can be realized through the UN. Unlike the League, the UN is based on the principle of universality because it symbolizes the longings among all peoples for the return of peace.[48] Thus Nehru, has total faith in the UN as an instrument of world government.

World Federation, Not Through Regional Association

Nehru felt that there is a great need of international order, of coming together of states in some form of cooperation. To him, national state alone is no longer adequate. It is too small a unit. A smaller state can not even maintain its independence on its own. It would be less capable to promote welfare to any great degree. Nehru, therefore, wants India's independence, within a global federation. In 1920s, he was reported to have said that 'once India was free he would favour a world federation, even to having India give up part of her independence to a larger group of which she is an equal member'.[49] Nehru calls for the World Republic and not an Empire based on the exploitation of one people by another. In 1930s, he wrote to his daughter, "the world is in a bad way and there seems to be no other way to get rid of its illness.[50]

In a letter to H.N. Spalding on May 22, 1940, Nehru wrote, "It is clear enough that there can be no independent small states in the future. There may possible be huge groups of states united together in each group and each group in a state of latent hostility, it is obviously a very undesirable possibility and it leads to no stability, but to future wars on a tremendous scale....the political and economic organization of the world must keep pace with technique of science, which has united the whole earth. That is to say that there should be a real

Commonwealth of interdependent states, each state foregoing that part of its independence which is necessary for the sake of this commonwealth or federation".[51]

Thus, Nehru seems to be against any form of regional, political or military organization as it leads to instability and war. He, however, does not mind regional organization based on economic consideration which must aim globalization rather than confined to only regional consideration. He never favours it as if represents only a limited number of state. The organization with limited representation will not solve the problem. On the contrary, it may even get in the way of the desperately needed global co-operation. Nehru instead proposes an idea of a world state with demilitarized nation-state, but with a police force.

In his address to the World Federalists Conference held in New Delhi in September 1963, Nehru gave his blueprint of World Federation. He said, "The world state among other things, must have a world police force... the state must be based on more or less demilitarized humanity, that is the present approach to arms and building up huge forces armaments must go".[52]

Nehru specifically maintains that, the initiative for the World Federation must be taken by the Great Powers so that the small and medium powers can join the venture. He also suggests an idea of 'federal legislature' to regulate the matters of common concern. And "each nation having autonomy within its borders and submitting international matters to the union legislature to which it send its representatives".[53]

No doubt, Nehru suggests to transform the entire environment within which the institution of nation-state has to function, but it does not mean that he does not want any change in the functioning of the nations themselves from within.

Institutional

As elaborated above, Nehru suggests that the nation-state system should function within the United Nations Organization. Thus, the entire international relations will be institionalized. In course of time, the UNO will function as a world government and the international anarchy will come to an end. If it happens, then the nation-state system will become a sub-set of the main society of man. Nehru says that it is not very difficult to do it at present when only few participators are powerful both militarily and economically. Only those few states will have to give up a perusal of narrow national interest. They have to cultivate enlightened national interests and submit themselves to the UNO or the common government of the world federation.

Strategy of Change for Individual

A new civilization calls for a new Man.[54] A new Man needs to be scientific minded person. It means he must have an inquiring mind. He should not accept anything without proper questioning and testing. He should be a rational man.

Moreover, a rational man must be fearless and frank. He should be free from false pride and prejudice. He must have the quality of tolerance. The tolerance can be cultivated provided one is broad minded. He should view his problems as a part of a larger good. He should not be selfish and narrow minded. Unless Man changes his mode of thinking, his attitude and behaviour can not be changed. If man does not change, scientific and technological boon may turn into curse and lead us to our dooms day.

In the society of mankind, Nehru expects everyone to enjoy a decent standard of living. It may be a modest standard, or a luxurious one. Secondly, it will be a world in which every individual, race, a no nation will be given equal opportunity to develop "good" life. The man race or nation will not exploit others. Man made obstacles for progress and prosperity will be ineffective. Thirdly, it will be a world in which each one will enjoy the basis right of freedom of self expression and development. Every one will, thus, live in society with enough opportunities to enjoy one will, thus, live in society with enough opportunities to enjoy a good standard of living as well as a good amount of freedom. These conditions will preserve the dignity of human being.

Nehru relates the question of the dignity of human being with the issue of justice in the world order. So long as the dignity of a common man is not preserved, no order can claim to be a just order. The just world order must preserve the dignity of the common human being in world society.

Nehru never wants an individual to turn his liberty and freedom into license. On the contrary he writes, "Freedom is always accompanied with responsibility. Freedom always entails obligation whether it is a nation's freedom or an individual's freedom".[55]

Hence, Nehru's concept of freedom implies social responsibility and, accordingly, a nation's political freedom is conditioned by international obligations. No justice can be realized in the world order of Nehru's vision unless these conditions are met with.

Like nations, men are divided by mutual hatred, fear, intolerance and hostility. They are afraid of each other. They hate each other in the name of religion, region and race. They fight for name and fame. They are irrational and subject themselves of passions. They can not see their larger interests and act in that direction. These are negative forces. They are prisoners of their self-created cultural confinements. Side by side, there are positive forces too like the forces of science and technology, which have capacity to bring people together. The distance between the nations has decreased. According to Nehru these forces need to be encouraged, and strengthened. These forces have potentiality to remove poverty and bring prosperity for all. They are capable of creating a new civilization which can be unique. Most of the problems of the old civilization like ignorance, disease, starvation, ill health and object poverty an be abolished by this new civilization. He knew that the new civilization will have its own new problems. But he is very much certain that virtues of the new civilization will enable man to resolve these new problems himself. But in order to create a new civilization, a new man needs to be cultivated. It can be done provided his values of life is changed.

Social Environment

How can a social and cultural environment be changed? - is a relevant question. Nehru believes that all cultural and social environments are in a constant process of change resulting from normal economic, social and political developments. Constant change is a law of life. The industrial revolution was a catalyst to the process of change. The major agents of change are reforms, campaigns, revolutions and wars, by which it can be instrumented.

Nehru emphasizes that environment as an agent of change play a more significant role more than an individual does. But he was not totally pessimistic about the role of an individual. Nehru urges that if attitude and behaviour of men can be changed by conscious efforts, it can give a boost to new civilization. According to Nehru, man takes a long time to change his attitude and behaviour as he is unable to control his passions, and elemental urges. Most of the time, we find that man is fatalist. He fears change and looks for security. He is essentially conservative in attitude. Hence the progress of new civilization will be painfully slow.

Individuals and states are not self-conscious and realist in assessing their ownselves. Mankind suffers from 'moral myopia'. Hence, they can not see the immorality of their own behaviour. On account of this 'moral myopia', the prospects for a better civilization are dim.[56]

To sum up. Nehru proposes three things to build a new world order; (i) new man; (ii) new leadership; and (iii) new culture.

To Nehru, "a new world requires a new kind of man, a man who is free from attachment, from any kind of hatred, from any kind of fear. A new world, a brave world, and a pretty generation do not go together".[57]

A New Leadership

According to Nehru, the new leadership with a new value system is a prerequisite. The role of a statesman in this disturbed world is to reduce tensions and conflicts. He feels that, through the application of science and technology, it is possible to reconstruct the social order so as to extend the fruits of modern civilization to one and all. Every state must have a conscience of its own and the nations like the individuals should also observe certain ethical standard or else their ultimate doom fall is inevitable. That is what a new leadership needs to understand and rise to the occasion.

New Culture

While accepting the honorary degree of Doctor of Law from the University of Ceylon in January 1960, Nehru elaborated his ideas on world culture. He said, "We should, by all means, adhere to our respective cultures, but there is something more than that national culture; it is human culture. Today it is more essential for us to develop that culture in a world culture. Otherwise the world will go to pieces. We must think in terms of a world culture. And if you want to prepare for that one world, you have to think of it, instead of growing in a narrow groove".[61]

As Nehru views, narrow culture and broad humanism can not co-exist. A new civilization will be a synthesis of many national cultures. We need to create a world culture which should not destroy mind and the spirit of man.

Nehru accepts that the main component of international society is a system of nation-states. They are the main actors who play a significant role in maintaining an order in the society. In the absence of the world government, the order in the society of states is maintained by a few powerful nations. Nehru resents it and advocates that the international society be democratised. Moreover, a few dominant powers are not united. They are competing with each other for capturing the world market. In order to perpetuate their exploitation, the dominant powers like England, France are practicing imperialism and colonialism. The other competing powers, like Germany, Italy and Japan are competing with them and are the in search of colonies. Such a game of power politics is dangerous for global peace. Small powers are treated only as pawns on the chess board of world politics.

People who were living in countries — powerful or weak — are politically, kept intact by a dose of narrow nationalism and by the principle of territorial sovereignty. Nehru firmly believed that the ideologies of imperialism and narrow nationalism can not nurture order in international society. They can not generate a just order at all under the circumstance. Hence he resents such an order.

Besides that, the present order encourages the politics of confrontation, rather than that of co-operation. Hence, the institution of war is in-built in that order. Nehru had warned the world against such an order before the outbreak of the Second World War. Even after the Second World War, the politics of confrontation continued. Only the main actors and ideologies changed. The eye ball to eye ball confrontation between the USA and the USSR after the Second World War, gave birth to the politics of Cold War. It was the most dangerous politics as it was played under the shadow of nuclear weapons. It would have brought total annihilation of life on the earth. The Repetition of such an old game of politics, even after the defeat of fascism and the victory of democratic forces, saddened Nehru.

In order to improve the functioning of the nation-state system, he suggests mainly two strategies: (1) the code of conduct in the form of Panchsheel for bilateral relations; and (2) the creation of the world federation for multi-lateral relations and for replacing the politics of confrontation by that of the politics of cooperation.

Nehru does not opt for transcending the nation-state system over night. He, however, does not mind it but knows that it will take a long time to do away with the three hundred year old system.

Nehru knows that the nation-states system too can't change unless the people (citizens) residing within it change themselves, their thinking, value-system and behaviour. Hence, he suggests that the individual within the nations need to change their culture by becoming conscious about their new environment which is totally changed by the forces of a new civilization - science and technology. The changed man through a new leadership with a new value system will ultimately change the environment within which nation-state functions. With a change in individual and his institution, i.e., a nation-state, a new global order based on justice and equality will be created and that will promise a permanent peace on the earth.

It is necessary to note that like his political guide, Gandhi, Nehru also emphasises the role of an individual in order to create an equitable world order and like him he chiefly operates on the level of intuition. It is striking to note that Gandhi's operation bears leaning towards philosophy, while Nehru's concern is mainly to co-relate the intuition within intellect and generate a rationalist point of view. Gandhi is a severe critic of western political practices while Nehru instead of criticising the west tries to incorporate scientific mode of thinking popular in the west with intuitive mode of thinking of the east. Nehru, however, does not suggest any new political processes to be initiated at national level, so that ultimately they would affect the change at the global level. This task is fulfilled by Lohia as he suggests a novel processes to create an equitable world order. Hence, we need to review Lohia's discourse on the global problematique of order and peace.

NOTES AND REFERENCES

1. Williard Range, *Nehru's World View : A Theory of International Relations*, University of Georgia Press, Athens, 1961, p. 44.
2. Gopal Sarvepalli (ed.), *An Anthology*, Oxford University Press, New Delhi, 1980, p. 494.
3. Ibid., p. 495.
4. Ibid., p. 631.
5. Ibid., p. 632.
6. Williard Range, Op.cit., No. 1, p. 47.
7. Jawaharlal Nehru, *The Discovery of India*, Asia Publishing House, 1966, p. 553.
8. Jawaharlal Nehru, Glimpses of World History, New York, pp. 4 and 182.
9. Jawaharlal Nehru, *Unity of India : Collected Writings, 1937-1940*, V.K. Krishna Menon, and L. Drumond (ed.), 1941, pp. 272-73.
10. Gopal, Op.cit., No. 2, pp. 422-23.
11. Jawaharlal Nehru, *Speeches of Prime Minister Jawaharlal Nehru*, Ministry of Information and Broadcasting, New Delhi, 1964, June 1945-February 1953, p. 386.
12. M.N. Das, *The Political Philosophy of Jawaharlal Nehru*, Allen and Unwin, London, 1961, p. 192.
13. A.P. Rana, "The Non-Hegemonial Imperative : The Non-Aligned Regulation of India's National Security Problematic and the

Universalisation of International Society, *The Indian Journal of Political Science*, 1991, vol. 4, No.1.

14. Jawaharlal Nehru, Op.cit., No. 7, pp. 542-44.
15. *Speeches of Prime Minister Jawaharlal Nehru*, Vol. June 1949-Feb ruary 1953 (1954), p. 143.
16. Williard Range, Op.cit., No. 1, p. 121.
17. Ibid., p. 122.
18. Ibid., p. 123.
19. A.P. Rana, *Imperatives of Nonalignment*, Macmillan, London, 1976, p. 51.
20. Williard Range, Op.cit., No. 1, p. 50.
21. Jawaharlal Nehru, Op.cit., No. 7, pp. 55-52.
22. Jawaharlal Nehru, *Glimpses of World History*, p. 402.
23. Ibid., pp. 490-91.
24. Gopal Sarvepalli, Op.cit., No.2, p. 300.
25. Ibid., p. 315.
26. Williard Range, Op.cit., No. 1, p. 69.
27. Ibid., p. 65.
28. Ibid., p. 65.
29. Gopal Sarvepalli, Op.cit., No. 2, p. 41.
30. Jawaharlal Nehru, *Glimpses of World History*, pp. 490-91.
31. Jawaharlal Nehru expressed this views in his presidential address to the Indian National Congress at Lahore session in December 1929, when the historic resolution of Poorna Swaraj was adopted.
32. Jawaharlal Nehru, *India's Independence and Social Revolution*, Vikas Publication, New Delhi, 1984, p. 9.
33. Gopal Sarvepalli, Op.cit., No. 2, pp. 381-82.
34. Williard Range, Op.cit., No. 1, pp. 1-18 (Nehru's views on the forces of new civilizations are discussed in detail).
35. Ibid., pp. 1018.
36. Ibid., pp. 6-7.
37. Jawaharlal Nehru, *Glimpses of World History*, p. 476.
38. Michael Breacher, *Nehru : A Political Biography*, New York, 1959, p. 99.
39. Jawaharlal Nehru, *Glimpses of World History*, pp. 173 and 202.
40. Jawaharlal Nehru, Op.cit., No. 2, p. 525.
41. Ibid., pp. 552-53.
42. Gopal Sarvepalli, Op.cit., No. 2, pp. 415-16.
43. Ibid., pp. 346-47.
44. Jawaharlal Nehru thought that the UN (like League) also will become

a generator of a climate of hostility, if it falls under the control of a particular bloc and then be used as an instrument against other states. Nehru therefore is a staunch defender of the right of veto in the security council abused as it might be, on the grounds that it is the chief obstacle to the prevention of the security council's falling under the control of one block. He considers the veto desirable also because it prevents the UN so often from resorting to the undesirable method of violence, and forces the UN to rely on peaceful procedures to settle disputes.

45. Gopal Sarvepalli, Op.cit., No. 2, p. 346.
46. Ibid., p. 168.
47. Ibid., p. 499.
48. Ibid., p. 169.
49. Williard Range, Op.cit., No. 1, p. 54.
50. Ibid., p. 54.
51. Gopal Sarvepalli, Op.cit., No. 2, p. 536.
52. Jawaharlal Nehru, *Speeches*, Vol. 4, p. 202.
53. Ibid., p. 347.
54. Williard Range, Op.cit., No. 1, p. 124.
55. Rafiq Zakaria (ed.), "A Study of Nehru", *The Times of India*, Bombay, 1960, p. 194.
56. Williard Range, Op.cit., No. 1, p. 14.
57. Quoted in S. Radhakrishnan, *Our Heritage*, Orient Paperbacks, 1973, pp. 130-131.
58. Radhakrishnan, "Liberation of Humanity", in Zakaria (ed.), "A Study of Nehru", *The Times of India*, Bombay, p. 88.

Chapter 4

LOHIA'S CONCEPTION OF INTERNATIONAL SOCIETY

Being a contemporary of Mahatma Gandhi and Jawaharlal Nehru, Ram Manohar Lohia like them, was reacting to the prevailing international political situation. His reactions are more systematic and studied. Basically, he begins his inquiry by asking the fundamental questions: what is the goal of the human life? why should we live in a society or a state? Lohia himself replies. The main goal of every individual in a society is to develop his personality fully. If that goal is not realized in that particular society, in Lohia's view, the order which sustains that society is inadequate. Hence we need to change that order. The same question is raised at the international societal level. Lohia's views on this issue are analyzed systematically in this chapter.

Ram Manohar Lohia (1910-1967) divides his views in three parts. In the first part, Lohia's conception of international society is discussed. Lohia agrees with Gandhi and Nehru, that the international society is basically composed of the nation-state. They are the dominant actors. They create order in international society. However, Lohia was thoroughly dissatisfied with that order, as he perceives that the society is highly stratified between the hegemon (powers) and the peripheral powers. In order to rectify that order, Lohia suggests a strategy. The second part discusses that strategy. Being an idealist, Lohia wants to do away with the unjust order and suggests a long-term strategy to transcend that order, so that the society of states can be transformed into a society of men. This strategy elaborated by Lohia for the global order and peace.

Nature and functioning of International Society : Organizing and Operational Principles

In Lohia's perception, international society is composed of two elements : (1) Nation-states and (2) Mankind. Lohia's perception seems to match Kant's conception on international society. He hopes, "...sooner or later, the whole world may become a federal state and the entire mankind, a political group".[1] Now let us examine what he has to say about the nature of the society composed of nation-state and orientation of mankind. In the later part, his strategy of transforming nation-states into federation and, mankind into a single 'political group' is discussed.

Hegemonial Powers

Lohia perceives international society as historically divided between the hegemonial powers and the peripheral powers. The society does not remain static as hegemonial nations keep on changing according to the cycle of history. According to him, the history moves cyclically. Once upon a time, Greeks and Romans were at the center of power. The United Kingdom and France were hegemons of the international society during the mid-war time. But in the post-second world war era, the hegemony shifted to the United States of America (USA) and the Union of Soviet Socialist Republic (USSR). Thus, the centre of power and prosperity derived from it go on shifting from one nation to another nation or one region to another region, over a period of time. But, this prosperity is unevenly distributed as the majority of states were deprived of what a few powerful states could obtain by virtue of their power (military and material). A nation or a group of nations have become prosperous themselves, and, thus hegemon in world politics. Though the cyclic motion of history may bring prosperity to other states — the movement of cycle will depend upon the wishes of hegemon and therefore Lohia was of the view that it would be necessary to break this dependence on cyclic motion if the entire mankind is to seek the benefits necessary for growth and prosperity.[2]

For Lohia, the dominant actors in international politics are nation-states. But whichever (nation) become the hegemon in the international society, never likes to give up its hegemony voluntarily. They decide their priority in accordance with their interest. They impose 'order' of their liking on the society. Historically, more and more nation-states have been emerging as independent actors in a society, but they have to accept, directly or indirectly, the domination of those few hegemon of the time.

In Lohia's time, the Cold War politics had divided the international society. Since this division had ideological overtones it did not remain confined to their respective positions within their own territorial limits (Soviet Union and the United States of America) —it affected many other countries in the world. International society reflected the sharp dividing lines through the foreign policy stance and in the formulation of domestic policies of many states. Lohia did not appreciate it among the countries of the Third World as it distorted the very concept of nationalism, nationhood and thereby the distinct identity of nation. International forces in the process affected the loyalty of the citizens as they could not resist the appeal of communism and capitalism. This was going too far and therefore Lohia wrote, "But in the world of nation-states, as it is today, if the basis of politics in not one's own state and its people, it is some other state, high priest of some or the other dream of future.... The entire politics in the country is divided among devotees of the different international temples, and the very concept of nationhood is clouded".[3]

Lohia further objects that due to Cold War, the autonomy of politics within the nation is adversely affected. Even though Lohia knew that the third world nations have become peripheral in the world politics, he did not blame the dominant nations for the gloomy state of affairs. He blamed the architects of the foreign policies of the non-aligned nations for such a situation. According to him, the non-aligned nations themselves are responsible for their peripheral position in the world politics.

Two Contradictory Systems

Ever since the two superpowers have extended their ideological conflict through military alliances (WARSAW Pact and NATO), they have been is search of 'power vacuums'. It would not be an exaggeration to say that the concept of power vacuum got into reckoning with the onset of the Cold War. With the overwhelming presence of the two superpowers, other nations had hardly any option in this regard as they could not challenge the conflicting claims and strategic interest of the two warring camps.

For Lohia is was quite distressing that the two superpowers were so much involved in their own conflict that they could hardly pay any attention to other serious problems with which the international society was afflicted. Many parts of the world were reeling under poverty, over population, civil wars, the problems of social and economic injustice and to all this the two superpowers were mute witnesses, despite their military and economic capabilities. These tension needed priority and attention over the Cold War dominated politics.[4]

Economic order in the existing international system perpetrates inequality and injustice which was far more disturbing for than the 'rich' and the 'poor' divide of nations. This system does not have any device to overcome this lacuna of the international society. To that extent, the existing international order is inadequate and calls for restructuring.

In order to dominate the existing structure of international politics and to seek more allies to their camp from the third world countries, the hegemon powers applied new devices to attract them to their camp. While commenting on the era of peaceful coexistence of Khrushchev-Kennedy (KK) time of the late sixties, Lohia dubbed it (peaceful coexistence) as yet another device to win over new allies to their side. To him, the doctrine of peaceful-coexistence was a rhetoric to disguise their ulterior motives. They (super powers) devised to seek from respite the tension of the Cold War when it becomes unbearable and disproportionate. Unbearable in terms of the cost involved in the senseless arms race - disproportionate for the Soviet Union as it could not match the United States Economic power.

The real peaceful coexistence could come about provided the two camps try to exist in such a way that a maximum capacity of every individual living on this earth could be utilized in the service of the humanity. Lohia calls it a stage of "approximation" in human development. The so-called Khrushchev-Kennedy peaceful co-existence did not ensure this objective. Hence, 'coexistence' was an empty doctrine. It was propounded to buy time to out pace each other in arms race. Lohia was of the view that the doctrine of peaceful coexistence could turn out to be an adequate one provided it was combined with approximation. His own conception of nonalignment rested on a very different premise where he wanted it to be an independent force against the two warring camps because then only the process of approximation could materialise.[5]

Lohia was convinced that the two camps can never co-exist in peace. The theory of peaceful coexistence' is a 'trick' or 'trap' of the two blocs to lull the third world countries to believe in them and too their line. The super powers even go to the extent of direct intervention in the internal affairs of a weak nation.

Interventionists

The dominant powers were interventionists. They intervene in the internal affairs of other nations, either 'imperialistically' or in the name of 'liberation'. But, their main aim was to pursue their national interests.

They never intervene for the good of the mankind or in the larger interests of the international society. This was not a new thing. According to Lohia, every hegemon has been intervening in the affairs of a peripheral powers and, thus, keeping its domination intact. It has been a continuous process and it is necessary to snap this continuity. The capability of dominant powers to intervene in the internal affairs of a nation creates a situation in which the international politics was monopolized by super powers. In order to break the monopoly of dominant powers, Lohia suggested twin strategies to improve the operation of the existing international order. These strategies will be discussed a little later.

Lohia on War

Unlike Hobbes, Grotius, Kant, Gandhi and Nehru, Lohia did not blame human nature for the outbreak of war. He presumed that, every human being was capable of developing his personality to the full extent, provided the necessary conditions were created.For outbreak of war, or the World War, he blames the system composed of nation-states and their ideologies of imperialism, colonialism, capitalism and the communism.

Lohia considers wars as products of injustice prevalent in the world. Every nation-state tries to get justice and that too only for its own nation. No one seeks justice for the entire mankind. In order to get justice for itself, the nations accumulate weapons and the different type of armaments. Lohia believed that even if "possible" equality (if not total equality) is created among the nations and within the nations, they will do away with the weapons. Equality can be created provided imperialism, colonialism and racial discrimination removed from the body politic of international relations. The phenomena of war could also be eliminated provided every individual is given an equal opportunity of self-realization.

The main problematiques of Lohia's world order was hunger, slavery and war. He calls them the "three monsters" of the present civilization. According to him, these three monsters stalk the world today as never before and their lengthening shadows were imperiling our order as appears to exist. Today's 'order' is divided into two parts: The Western World and the Eastern World. One part of the world (west) is powerless to conserve what it has created and the other finds it difficult to create what it needs. Lohia thinks that some nations are determined to hold the master's right to make war. They hold the right to make war mainly because they are hegemon and the power was concentrated at few centres. The concentration of powers poses a threat of war as it gives birth to militarism and authoritarianism. Hence he suggests decentralization of power in order to eliminate war. The East (Asia) for too long had suffered slavery which made them poor and weak. This area needs to be relieved from poverty and slavery and, thus, needs to reconstruct that area for the world order. The world order based on peace and justice can be created provided international society is democratized.

Lohia on Political Processes at International Level

Lohia resents the absence of political process at global level in order to address the global problems. He wanted that some political processes should be initiated at the global level and the initiative should be taken by the great powers as well as by the third world countries. These processes may be initiated within a nation-state, but its impact will be felt at the global level. He suggests the following political processes for creating a global society consisting of mankind.

Novel Political Processes

Lohia opines that no genuine world order based on equality and justice can be created, unless world-wide political processes are generated. In order to generate those processes, he suggested four novel programmes as models of political process to take care of equitable development of mankind as a whole :

1. All the political parties in all the nations should adopt a hundred or fifty year programme about what type of change they envisage in the world.[7] Lohia wanted all the political parties to adopt the programme of international policy. He thought that the world was basically diseased in its international relationships. Its foundations have weakened. New, and more solid foundations were required to be laid. Hence, all the political parties all over the world need to have international policy regarding the future of the world. Lohia, views the basic function of the political parties would be to change the behaviour and the minds of men, throughout the globe. Hence they are obliged to adopt positions on international societal issues.
2. The super powers of the world like, the USA and the USSR - should also hold regular summit conferences to consider the problem of poverty and disarmaments and the methods of eradicating them.[8] In Lohia's view, the disarmament and abolition of poverty are two sides

of the same coin. War will never cease to be a threat to the mankind, unless poverty is eradicated from all over the world. He believed that, so long as inequality between the rich and the poor nations is not removed the idea of the world being a habitation for a single international family will remain a dream. He suggested the initiation of global political process by the rich nations, so that an equitable global society may be created.

3. A novel institution at global level like the World Development Authority may be conceived. Its main thrust should be economic reconstruction of the world economy. The World Development Authority may have objectives to improve agriculture as well as industries. This authority can organize pool of resources and skill from each nation of the world.
4. In order to make the unity of mankind a reality at the global level, Lohia suggests the fourth model of political process which he evolves from the reality of his time. In his time, many non-governmental peace movements were going on in many countries. These movements were fragmented and not co-ordinated. Moreover, these movements centered around the human problems and yet those movements were not effective to unite the human race. Hence, Lohia pleaded for a serious effort to federate them and institutionalize them and operate them in the form of civil disobedience movement at a global level.[9] Thus, Lohia wanted these International Non-Governmental Organizations (INGO) to wake up people from slumber and inspire them to protest against the vices through the Gandhian technique of *satyagraha.* He had a plan to translate the Gandhian ideas to suit at international societal level. Lohia maintained that hitherto, we have tried to bring about unity of mankind through religious and other ideological means in which we have failed. Now this can be effectively undertaken only through international political processes.

Lohia's Concept of Justice

Lohia had a theoretical mind and he evolves a coherent theory of justice in his ideology of "New Socialism"[10] for internal political life as well as for international relations. This project is confined to Lohia's consideration for international relation hence it tries to conceptualize only Lohia's views on justice in relation to international politics. Lohia wanted that the socialist doctrine be retold in terms of the simple truth that all men are equal, not only within the nations but also among nations. Thus, his concept of justice concerns "equality of man" everywhere and emancipation of man from war, hunger, starvation, slavery and poverty.[11] His conceptualization of justice emerges from his insight into the world history. In his, "Wheel of History", Lohia interprets human history as a tussle between crystallized castes and loosely cohesive classes. He writes, "castes represent conservative forces of stagnation, inertia and prescriptive right, while classes stand for a dynamic force of social mobilization". All human history, to Lohia, had been "an internal movement between castes and classes". This internal tussle of history will go on till the evil in man and society as not prevented from breeding. He expected, "the world might, through intelligent design, try to achieve a multi-coloured harmony of human race".[12] Thus, this concept of justice embodies in it, a "multi-coloured harmony". Lohia hoped that when equality of man and harmony amongst them is established, it will change its traditional forms on practically every major fronts. "In the place of an increasing standard of living within national frontiers, decent and minimum living standards for all men in the world will be assured. In the place of the alternatives between parliamentary and insurrectionary action, a balanced mixture of constitutional action and civil resistance, wherever necessary and possible, will be followed or practiced. In the place of an international organization of unequal members, a committee of nations, equal in membership and executive and based on some sort of adult franchise, will be established and maintained. In fact, socialism must first achieve the union of mankind in the mind before it can translate that into practice.[13]

Writing on the concept of justice, Lohia maintains that seven type of revolutions are going on in the world today to bring about justice. These revolutions are : (1) for equality between man and woman; (2) against politics, economic and spiritual inequality based on skin colour; (3) against inequality of backward and high groups or castes based on long tradition, and for giving special opportunities to the backward; (4) against foreign enslavement and for freedom and world democratic rule; (5) for equality and planned production and against the existence of and attachment for private capital; (6) against unjust encroachments on private life and for democratic methods; and (7) against weapons and for *satyagraha*.[14]

Lohia's concept of justice springs from the philosophy of humanism. His orientation of justice neither sacrifices the interest of the individual, nor of the society, and neither of the nation nor of the international society. It seeks a compromise between conflicting interests of individual, society and state.

Justice in International Society

Elaborating his ideas of international justice, Lohia points out the gray areas of injustice. Injustice prevails in international order mainly because 'injustice' is in-built in the order itself. International order is composed of nation-state system and ideologies of communism and capitalism. Both features divide nations and create tensions between them. Both these generate war, and economic inequality. In order to remove anomaly from the international order and to preserve 'peace', the international institution like the UNO was created. But in reality, the UNO instead of removing injustice perpetuates status-quo of the high politics of international reality. This reflects the existing reality of power politics and does not help mitigating injustice from the body politics of international order.

The UNO does not offer membership to every nation of the fact that the nation has a sovereign authority. Denying of membership on grounds of character of the government leads to confused partisanship and intrigues. It leads to injustice, as it discriminates nations. In order to create a sense of justice among the members of the UNO, "membership of the United Nations must be obtainable to every nation that has a government able to control its affairs".[15] According to Lohia, the principle of universalism must necessarily inhere in the United Nations.

Referring to the system of the UNO of 'one nation-one vote', Lohia appreciated the equality in law, but he criticizes that in reality, this principle was not observed due to the veto-system. He sought equality, not only in law, but also in its implementation.

Lohia believes that, if justice has to prevail in international society, the UN must acquire universal membership and put a step to the convention of the Veto power for class of permanent members within UNO.[16]

Justice and World Order

Lohia's concept of justice in world order was based on the twin concepts of the "Unity of Mankind" and "Equality of Man".

Unity of Mankind

Lohia was firmly convinced that the approximation (full development of human personality) of human race was not possible with the existing concept of international relationship. He, therefore, favoured a new idea of people to people relationship in place of government to government relationship which dominates the international affairs today. Every one has been striving for the unity of mankind. This strivings have been expressed through the need of one God, or one world or even oneness of all animal life. According to Lohia, aspiration for unity of Godhead was intimately connected with the aspiration for the political unity of mankind.[17] Lohia himself confesses that, the idea of unity of mankind was logical, but can not be reality. He was hopeful that, it will become reality as political process for their implementation starts. Lohia points out various world-wide movements going on in the different countries: "Ban the Bomb", Ban Inequality. These movements are not effective or are incapable of uniting the human race together because, they don't have programme of civil disobedience. Lohia pleads for a serious effort to federate them, to institutionalize them and to operate them through civil disobedience. He thought that while federating these movements, they will have an introspective outlook out of compulsion.[18]

Equality

Justice, even in world order, can not be achieved without the establishment of equality of man in that society. He writes that all those who desire for world peace through the world government must aspire to achieve a world view of equality against class or caste or regional inequalities.

Lohia conceives equality not only within a nation but also among nations and that such equality must not be limited to the field of law. The concept of equality must embrace economic, political and social and other areas also. Material equality among nations appears more difficult to achieve than material equality within the nations. No nation can, for long, remain equal within its frontiers if it is unequal against other nations. As water finds its level, human society tends to approximate its lowest levels. Provided these levels are otherwise not raised.[19]

For prevailing injustice, Lohia blames the existing international political and economic structure and pleads for its reshaping. Efforts should be to redesign the structure in such a way that the gap within and among nations can be bridged. Apartheid among the blacks and the whites was also a scar on humanity and to end such racial discrimination, Lohia advocated Satyagraha at international level. He however, did not elaborate the method of launching satyagraha at the international level.[20]

For Lohia, equality and liberty are inseparable. They are not in conflict. A world order in which men are given an equal opportunity of self-realization is a world having liberty and justice. He defines injustice as lack of equality and liberty that it is due to injustice and inequality that nation needs weapons and armaments. Lohia points out, "actually weapons mean injustice. Weapons are either meant to eliminate injustice or to reduce its intensity and that is why if injustice is totally eliminated there will be no need for armaments.[21] The weapons will not be necessary provided international society is reorganized on the basis of justice. According to him, inequality is the main element of various forms of injustice prevalent in human society. Hence 'if a society ever reaches the stage of possible equality, if not total equality, a stage might be reached for doing away with the weapons'.[22]

Lohia views equality in four aspects, viz., inward and outward as well as spiritual and material. He pleads for an integrated approach. He advocated, "Equality must therefore, be grasped in all its four meanings. Material equality must mean the outward approximation among nations as well as the inward approximation within the nation. Spiritual equality must mean upward kinship as much as it means inward equanimity, kinship, material equality within the nation and among nations is worthy to become a supreme aim of life and its purpose".[23]

By individual liberty in world order Lohia means unfettered freedom to move to die or live in any part of the world. Lohia advocates perfect freedom to anyone to settle anywhere one liked. The present rules and regulations for citizenship attached to the idea of one's territory are condemned by Lohia as outdated and barbarous. Lohia therefore had desired to travel through-out the world without a passport.[24] He writes, "Man's right to travel, work and die anywhere in the world should be recognized and laws of restrictions on travel and stay on grounds of indigen or undesirability should be also lashed. Citizenship should as much be a matter of intention and cultural loyalty as of birth or residence".[25]

Lohia's concept of justice also implies an urge to end all forms of colonialism and political rule of one nation over another. He considers colonialism as a shame to mankind and a serious impediment to the growth of an equal world. In the preface to Marx, Gandhi and socialism, Lohia writes, "National freedom is on the way to becoming men's irremovable property.... No people shall now be allowed to exercise direct rule over another. Indirect control, oppressions may continue and their fate shall be part of the wider fate of the total fight against injustice.

But direct political rule of one nation over another belongs to the irrevocable past".[26]

He, however, stands for further fight against injustice in an era of neocolonialism (indirect rule). He pleads that it is not the government but the people of the world must learn to fight whenever and wherever human rights are abused. Violation of human rights, no matter where they take place, should arouse warm sympathy with the victims and indignation against the tyrant.[27]

Methods for Acquiring Justice

Lohia goes beyond the areas of injustice, by also suggesting methods to fight out injustice. Before the method of Satyagraha was evolved, only two methods were popular, parliamentary and insurrectionary. But Lohia insists on Mahatma Gandhi's method of Civil-Disobedience or Satyagraha. He pleads its operationalization on a permanent basis on a world scale as it embodies direct action against any type of injustice. He writes, "for the first time in the world, the weapon of civil disobedience which had been in use by great man from Socrates to Thoreau was put into the hands of whole masses of men by Mahatma Gandhi".[28] Gandhi's weapon of satyagraha was used chiefly for political purposes, but now it should also be used for economic and social reformation. He further says, "a day may come later when the whole nation is summoned to organize resistance against injustice and for the achievement of a new order'.[29]

Thus, Lohia's points of departure in his concept of justice in the world order are the unity of mankind and equality. The unity of mankind can come through political process. We have so far tried to achieve this unity through religious and other ideological means. It can come through by uniting (or federating) international movements undertaken separately in different countries.

The second ideal of equality also can be achieved provided the entire world must conceive it. On creating the world view of equality, we will find the reasons for the prevailing inequality. Lohia blames the economic and political structure of the world for it. By giving an example, he points out that nation are producing weapons because there prevails inequality among them. An humble beginning is suggested by Lohia in the form of eliminating the idea of citizenship, which restricts man's movement. Man, therefore, can not develop his personality. The curtailment of liberty means curtailment of equality. It generates injustice for ever in the world.

Lohia's Twin Strategies to Reform the Functioning of the Existing Order

For Lohia, the existing international order is a victim of neo-colonialism and international imperialism practiced by the two power blocs. Hence, international order needs to be liberated from the twin grip of neo-colonialism and imperialism. Lohia suggests two strategies to liberate the international order: (1) The creation of the Third Camp; and (2) Strengthening of the international institution, i.e., the United Nations Organization. Thus, Lohia opts for power approach and institutional approach to improve the functioning of the international order.These two approaches are examined in detail below.

The creation of the Third Camp

According to Lohia the existing international order is status-quoist. It functions in the interests of the power blocs. What is needed is a restructuring of that order. The restructuring of the international order can be done by acquisition of 'power' by the nonaligned nations if it is delegated willingly. The non-aligned nations, therefore, should come together ideologically, economically and strategically. They must evolve an ideology of the Third World i.e., anti-military camps. They should not cooperate with or give in to the super powers. The non-aligned, if united, can stand apart and against the super powers. The non-aligned must learn to dictate terms to them. Lohia is against the so-called "independence of the two blocks", or a position of neutrality between them. It sounds good in principle but in reality it does not serve any purpose of national or international interest (peace). By adopting non-alignment, they sometime 'appease' one power and sometimes other. This amounts to aligning with either of the powers. In this way, non-aligned powers do not preserve their independence but surrender it to either of the powers. What is necessary to do, is to compel these super powers to work for world peace and economic justice for the entire world. In fact, when they act to serve their national interest, either by neutrality of the non-aligned or sometimes by alignment with either of the super power, it does not serve the purpose of the non-aligned nation. On the contrary, it serves the purpose of the super powers.[30]

Economically, the super powers are adopting anti-third world policy. It is being experienced by the Third World countries from time to time, and yet they do not learn the lesson. They must get united and form a third camp as they have their own community of interests. The super powers are dictating terms of trade on them, instead the non-aligned should do it. The fact is that the super powers are dependent on many 'commodities' which are available in the non-aligned nations. It does not happen. The non-aligned powers are incapable of dictating therms as they lack unity. At present, the non-aligned powers are more passive in asserting their status on international scene. Lohia says, in order to be successful, "it must become creatively independent". To quote him, "the third camp must not be an empire, but a participator in international events, because it will never be able to judge issues until it learns to play a part in their maturing".[31] Lohia wants Nehru's India to take initiative in bringing to the foreground the issues of economic reconstruction and, thus, help restructuring the international order.

Lohia advocates that, the Third World countries should come together militarily also. The military unity will yield power against the unjust super powers. But Lohia warns against military intervention by the non-aligned nation into the other non-aligned nations, which would otherwise be imperialistic intervention. He, however, advocates non-military intervention by the third camp in the non-aligned nation. To Lohia, such intervention is preferable to the by the super powers. In order to get maturity and to obtain desired results, the third camp must learn to intervene in the affairs of the countries of the third camp whenever "democracy" and "freedom" are threatened in any of its constituent territories, it must do everything to encourage and assist the growth of democracy and socialism in all those areas".[32] Thus, Lohia's ideas of the third camp are unique in character.

The third camp must stand for and advocate the idea of international law against the idea of naked power-play. The two camps may stand for 'power' and disregard the role of international law. They may stand for war. The third camp must stand for positive peace. To Lohia, peace is not the antithesis of war and so it is not a negative concept. Lohia pleads for some assertive action by the third camp. The third camp must learn to unite the world under the rubric of international law than on a consideration of 'self-interest'. This rivalry must discontinue. The passive non-alignment can not break it. Lohia holds that, "the third camp must indeed strive to do all it can to avoid war but it must also concern itself equally with the building up of such strength as will be adequate to open a new era in world relations.[33] This new ear of world relations can be built by creating a consensus on acceptance of international law by all the nations of the system.

The third force, can, at present, coordinate international peace movements. He writes, "I should think that the third camp has its immediate work in the fields such as the various types world unity movements, which are not attached to either of these two blocs, the international socialist movement, in particular its Asian Wing, and cultural or no-war movements unaffiliated to either bloc. The United Nations is also not be completely discarded. Several of its activities and agencies are such in which the third camp can gainful take part... It may also seek to combine all the world on such projects as a world development cooperation, international projects of reconstruction and peace and a world food pool".[34]

According to Lohia the present nonalignment by definition is a doctrine of subsidiary behaviour. The non-aligned nations can only affirm or deny what the principal actors of the world drama, US or USSR do or say. Thus, non-alignment is a doctrine of reaction.[35] In other words, it stands for passive neutrality. Lohia's concept of 'third camp' is not based on passive neutrality but on active neutrality. Clarifying that his concept is based on active and assertive neutrality, Lohia points out, "The neutral bloc is today only passively independent. It must become creatively independent. Its pretension to judge each issue on its merit will ever be hollow until it learns to put something of its own into the issues as they arise.... Neutrality that is based on national selfishness or passive waiting on events is inconsistent with the world view. To keep one's own country out of war is something wholly different from keeping war out of the world. The former is passive neutrality arising out of national selfishness while the latter is active neutrality arising out of a world view".[36]

Duties of the Third Camp

Lohia assigns a number of duties to the Third Camp:

a. to facilitate and complete the liberation of the colonial people of Africa and Asia;
b. to combat defence pacts and the peace preparations of the Atlantic and Soviet camps, which in reality are war pacts and preparations of war;
c. to annihilate the nefarious effects of the policy of armed appeasement undertaken by these camps;
d. to strive to make the UNO, through effective influence and constructive contribution, capable of realizing its role as an instrument of world peace and progress and, thus, to prevent this

organization from being used by the two power blocks as an arena of disputes, a clearing house of international rivalries and a syndicate of selfish interests; and

e. to promote and to consummate regrouping and the cooperation of all peoples and nations through a world government and, thus, prevent regrouping of people under war banner of the two power blocs.[37]

These duties can not be performed by the non-aligned nations as their minds are not liberated from the politics of two camps. He writes, "to liberate the human mind from the octopus grip of the two camps is to build up this new federation of the mind".[38]

Replying to the critic of the third camp as a camp without military power, Lohia writes, "what the third camp needs today is not so much military power as the power of faith, unshakable and unbearable faith".[39] As a clarification he stresses the need for a constructive approach to world problems. According to Lohia, what is needed now is to set up a virile federation of the mind. To emphasize his point, he writes, "Arms are a concentrated expression at least partly of a virile attitude. What is needed now is to set up a virile federation of the mind".[40] Lohia, thus, emphasizes the role of the political will, rather than its instrument i.e. the military power.

To Lohia, the existing international order does not function in the interest of all the nations. It works in favour of the USA and USSR. They wield power not only because they are militarily powerful but they are united ideologically and economically. They think in terms of their military security only. First of all, they have faith in themselves. They have political will to get things done. The non-aligned nations do not have that will because they are not united. They have not created a united front of their own. As they are not united, they can not create a united front. They think that it can not be created unless they have military power. Lohia is very much clear that the non-aligned needs military power as much as it needs a power of faith, unshakable and unbearable faith in itself which is lacking in the non-aligned movement today. Lohia, thus, suggests to confront the bi-polar world of injustice with the will to resist them and not to be their line. Thus, Lohia understands power as coming from the will to resist and, never from the barrel of a gun.

According to Lohia, ideas rule the world and the human life is wasted if he does not try to achieve "ought" (ideal) in life. The ideal which the non-aligned nations want to achieve is always reflected in its world view. They want to liberate today's world from war and destruction. They can not prove so by just adopting so-called non-alignment policy. It can be done only by creating the third camp of the non-aligned nations. The idea of the formation of the third camp itself will prevent any non-aligned nation joining the war banner of either of the camps. Again, the formation of the third camp itself generate power. The third camp will enforce approximation if they (two camps) themselves do not agree to approximate to each other as there will be parity amongst them; first, camp, second camp and third camp.

The two camps propagate that they believe in peaceful coexistence. But they do not experiment genuinely to co-exist but they buy time for military preparation. They will learn to co-exist only when they are forced to do so. It is possible, provided the third camp acquires enough strength to force the two blocks to coexist.

The main aim of the third camp is to obtain peaceful and just international order. The two rival camps are striving for negative peace, which means postponement of war. Lohia thinks that, the creation of the third camp will help avoiding war and create a new international order based on positive peace.

Empowering the UNO : Institutional Approach

According to Lohia, the international institutions like the United Nations Organization (UNO) or (the League of Nations) are created to bring about stable and lasting peace. Instead, an organization like the UNO is used by the two power blocks as an arena of dispute, 'a clearing house of international interests'. Lohia believes that the League of nations had failed for the same reason. By pointing out the successive failure of the League is case of Ethiopia in 1935, Spain in 1936 and China in 1937, Lohia maintains that this failure proved costly for the world. According to Lohia, along with the rising tide of armaments it destroyed the international order which was created after the First World War.[41] The UNO which was established after the Second World War with so much of presumptions and high aims seems to be walking on the same footing as its predecessor.

To Lohia, the functioning of the UNO is a great disappointment. It came into existence to serve the mankind with a concrete solution of a stable and lasting peace. Instead the UNO itself has become an arena of struggle between the two dominant power blocs. The member of nations are supposed to be guided by universal interest while evaluating any international issue. In practice they are guided by their own national interest. The guiding principle of national interest has rocked its noble aims and high proclamations. The member nations have forgotten the basic truth that in order to make any institution successful for internationalism, they should surrender some part of their sovereignty. The UNO failed to make them realize that nations do not belong only to nation states, but from a part and parcel of the whole human race.[42]

Lohia suggests three dimensional strategy for transformation of the UNO as it can not help in obtaining the idea of world peace with its present weaknesses. He suggests strategies for turning the United Nations from being a clearing house of international intrigues to a repository of the collective conscience of mankind.[43]

Lohia has a great hope to achieve world peace through the UNO. Inspite of its inherent weaknesses, he still hopes that it can achieve peace, provided the organizational and procedural defects of the UN charter be removed. He suggests the following:

1. Membership of the UNO be expanded;
2. The permanent seats in the security council be removed; and
3. The right of Veto be taken away.[44]

Pleading for the universal membership of the UNO, he writes, "Membership of the United Nations must be obtainable to every nation that has a government able to control its affairs. Denial of membership on grounds of character of the government must inevitable lead to confused partisanship and intrigues".[45]

Being a politician, Lohia knows that the permanent seats and the Veto are only a reflection of existing realities of power. For Lohia, it is not a just arrangement. Justice demands that equality in law as well as in fact should be sought. Judicial equality always precedes factual equality. Comparing the provision of restricted Veto power of the UNO with the caste system of India, Lohia writes, "Permanent seats and the Veto are an expression of the division of the world into great powers and small and therefore of an odious international caste system; restrictions on membership result in the nefarious black-balling of new tantrums for the sake of narrow interest".[46] He further says that, "a judgment by the security council, four or five of whose members sit in perpetuity, is always open to doubt and challenge. The UN, therefore, must acquire universal membership end the Veto and, the permanent seats.

Lohia expresses his great dissatisfaction with the UNO and dubs it as the most artificial institution. To Lohia, the UNO must represent the conscience of the mankind. It will not be so unless the UNO is reorganized on the basis of the adult franchise. Lohia treats the UNO as a stepping stone to the future world government. But meanwhile he seeks revision of the charter of the UNO. According to Lohia, the UNO will not become an effective and acceptable instrument for reconstruction and defence of the world unless the charter of the UNO reflects universality and equality of membership. It should be reorganized in such a way that, no nation or no people would think it worthwhile to challenge its authority. Like law courts and national parliaments, the decisions of the United Nations must also be unchallengable and binding. Such a situation can come about only if, nation are equally willing to share their sovereignty in the larger interest of mankind. The UNO can be an effective instrument in identifying areas of common interest over which consensus can be arrived at. So long as it is not done, it will remain an inefficient institution to bring peace, order and justice in international society.

MANKIND AND THE TRANSFORMING STRATEGY

In the first part, Lohia's views on the 'system change' (Nation-State System) have been examined. Even after suggesting a strategy for the change of the system, Lohia is not satisfied with his solution. To him, it is a half-way solution. He knows it will not improve the functioning of a society of states; it will not solve the problems of civilization.

According to Lohia, we have been passing through a civilizational crisis. The main point of crisis is that this civilization has rendered itself incapable of awakening the entire human race. True civilization must help every individual to evolve a culture of outward activity and inward poise and, thus, a man can blossom his personality fully and totally. The present civilization can not address this problematique seriously mainly because, the entire mankind is divided by the nation-states. The society composed of nation-states divide people in the name of sovereignty, ideology and nationhood. At present, the interest of the nation-state clashes with the interest of the global society of men. Hence there has been tension between "what is' and "what ought to be". This tension has been persisting because we live in a society composed of nation-states. Lohia writes, "Rarely have national interest and world interest coincided to this degree".[47] Man needs to think to come out of this imprisoning system but man has ceased to think and is afraid of exploring new realms of living and thought. Nevertheless Lohia writes, "To attain a world order, therefore, is to build a new civilization to resume the onward journey of the mind and to attempt a fresh arrangement of life".[48]

Nation-State System and Ideologies

Today's nation-state system operates through mainly two European ideologies — Capitalism and Communism. These ideologies are status-quoist and do not want any change. He believes that the liberation of mankind and world unity can be achieved neither on the basis of the communist system nor on the ground of capitalist considerations. Both of them are irrelevant for this purpose.

According to Lohia, the existing civilization propagated by the West and the Russians (capitalism versus communism) can not be valid for the whole of mankind as it is biased and regional. These ideologies to not promise full development of personality. Hence, Lohia conceives a new ideology of socialism. (Some ideas blended with Gandhism). He dreams socialism in the form of a free from all types of exploitation - social, economic and political. Lohia's socialism is based on humanistic foundations in which the interests, the individual of the society, of the state, or of the world are never sacrificed. To him, all men are equal and they should form a single world of free association in doctrine as well as in foreign policy.

Lohia, thus, visualizes the ideology of socialism, instead of capitalism or communism, as capable of building a world order. Secondly, he thinks that the forces of socialist ideology will break the nation-state system and the world parliament will be created out of the United Nations Organization.

Factors to Create World Community

Lohia enumerates several factors to create a global community, but mainly, he blames the existing ideologies (capitalism/communism) of the nation-state system. He calls it a civilizational crisis. As for Lohia, socialism is a creed of change and justice while capitalism and communism are inextricable tried up in the meshes of an old and dying world. The twin ideologies of the present world, capitalism and communism, promise to create a world order based on human equality and justice. But in fact, they breed poverty, inequality and fear in the world. Let us therefore understand the nature of the crisis.

According to Lohia, these ideologies do not unite the humanity. On the contrary they divide them in two parts — capitalist world and communist world. Both of them promise to create a world order based on equality among people by full development of human personality. But, both of them have failed to develop human personality to full extent because these ideologies have divided man on the earth.

Emancipation of Humanity Through Full Development of Human Personality

The present civilization helps developing only "maximum efficiency" and not the "total efficiency": of man. Lohia is convinced that, neither communism nor capitalism is valid principles for the change over maximum to total efficiency. He writes, "Communism has indeed talked of a world order based on equality among the nations and the full development of human personality, both to arise out of the abolition of exploitation. But these general ideals are as deceptive and meaningless as the earlier ones of capitalism which has talked of a world order arising out of perfect competition. Neither doctrine has tried to translate these general wishes into concrete ideals".[49]

This has happened because the wheel of history moves like a cycle. It has moved because, new ideas are always tried by a particular nation within the boundaries of a nation.

The civilizational crisis repeats itself in history because every society is subject to some law of change. It has its own mechanism of internal as well as external motion of law. Internally, every society (nation-state) is busy achieving maximum efficiency for its own people and not 'total efficiency' for the whole of mankind. The communist and capitalist doctrines boast about the welfare of the entire mankind, but work only for the citizens of their respective states. In practice, these doctrines produce a 'chosen people' within the humanity. Hence they divide the world between 'chosen people' (people of the nation) and the people outside the circle.[50] It has remained plight of every civilizations produced by history and no civilization has ever taken the task of full development of personality of every human being.

External Law of Motion

To Lohia, the history is a narration of struggle among nations to get supremacy in international society. The class which comes to power within a nation, strives to get supreme role for its nation in international society. He maintains, like Toynbee, that a civilization 'disrupts' or 'stagnates' under the pressures of internal and external struggle. Hence, the history delineates a story of an external shift of prosperity and power from one region to another. Once upon a time, the Greek and Romans were powerful, while England and France were powerful before the Second World War and in the post-Second World War era, the USSR and USA have been dominating powers. Thus, the centre of prosperity and power keep shifting from one nation or region to another in course of time. But the fact is that the entire mankind has never become prosperous. A nation or a group of nations enjoy prosperity at the cost of other nations or group of nations. Such the motion of history moves, according to Lohia, in a cyclic way.[51]

Lohia further explains that internal and external laws of motion are interrelated. 'With the external increase in power and prosperity, internal inequality decreases; whereas with decrease in such power, internal inequality increases.[52]

Each nation, when it thinks only from the nation's point of view, tries to rise in power in its relationship to the outside world. It strives for better living and greater equality within the state. In course of time, one nation becomes powerful than others and thus, wheel of history goes on. Thus, obviously dominant factor in the world history is the shift of power and prosperity from one region to another. No nation thinks in terms of the welfare of the entire humanity. This thinking is justified by the existing ideologies, hence the civilizational crisis.

In order to overcome this civilizational crisis, Lohia suggests that the nation-state's ideological systems should be guided by the principle of "total efficiency" of the individual instead of "maximum efficiency". Hitherto all the civilizations have been guided by the principle of `maximum efficiency'. If this barrier is removed the nation-state system can be broken.

We need to create a new civilization which should be guided by the twin principles:

1. to achieve 'total efficiency' for the whole of mankind; and
2. to develop total personality of an individual. Unless mankind achieves human approximation through an attempt of total efficiency instead of maximum efficiency, the wheel of history will not stop.

The existing institutions of nation-states and doctrines of Marxism and capitalism can not help us. To stop this external shift and internal oscillation, Lohia wants such a universal doctrine, which will regulate this regional shift of power from one country to another or from one continent to another. To stop this cycle of history, efforts are needed. History by itself will not do so as it has no automatic motion. The present thinking that capitalism or communism will arrest the process of history be given up. They are incapable to do so.

Reasons for Capitalist Incapability

The present civilization is predominantly Euro-centric. It has its dual forms, capitalism and communism and it is incapable of bringing the entire world within its folds. On the contrary it produces poverty, fear and war. "...these two systems have been unable to alleviate even by a small measure these three poisonous portions of mankind, poverty, war and fear"[53]

To Lohia, the 'Atlantic' and the Soviet camps reflect only a split of the European civilization. But for Lohia split is not a new development. Even before, when a civilization had matured and when it was about to decay, it tended to split in order to regenerate itself. The entire world, however has shaken with this split but there was nothing in the split which would have been of concern to the whole of mankind. To the outside world, capitalism and communism seem to be fighting a deadly war for their principles, but in reality, they are busy raising national output and increasing standard of living within their national territories. Capitalism does so in the name of 'perfect competition' in a democratic set-up of government, while communism under a totalitarian regime. Neither of these doctrines, however, has concretely concerned itself with the two basic issues of total efficiency and total personal development in respect of the whole mankind as well as individual.[54]

Science and Technology

Besides, this civilization stands for the application of science to industry and agriculture. It strives for increasing national output collectively and increasing living standard individually. It propagates social equality and peace in the world.[55] Lohia it is a pseudo claim and it can never bring equality or world peace. According to him, the present civilization has reached its dead end. It can not be spread all over the world, as its technology is incapable of repetition in Asia and Africa due to their peculiar circumstances. The Western powers could develop mainly because they had colonies to exploit. But, this circumstance does not prevail in Afro-Asian countries. Lohia points out 'too little land and too many men and too few tools are a mark of Asia, so the application of the technique of mass production is utterly impossible'.[56] It is, therefore, incapable to produce the desired world order based on economic equality.

Old Agreement and Treaties

Without specifying any international agreement and treaties, Lohia writes, "Old treaties and agreements and the procedures connected with them further hamper the birth of a new order". Colonialism and imperialism of the West perpetuated in Africa also come in the way for creating a world order. Lohia appeals to the people of world and particularly Asians to join with the Africans in their national struggle for human equality and justice 'through massive international brigades of *satyagrahis* or nonviolent resisters'.[57]

Not to Judge Every Issue on Merits

Lohia appeals the non-aligned nations to pursue a policy independent of both the camps and not to judge issue as it arises, on merit. To Lohia, both the camps (USA/USSR) are imperialists and they do not stand for new world order based on justice. By judging the issue in an isolated way, it results in rendering of alternate service to the two camps. Thus the non-aligned help them to perpetuate the old order.[58]

The world order must opt for a dynamic and positive peace. Actually in Lohia's view, "the essential function of world order is to secure peace".[59] He says, peace is of two kinds - positive peace and negative one. Positive peace is "inherent in and the result of an appropriate manner of life". While the negative peace refers to "mere postponement of war achieved through diplomatic pressures and threats and the force of organized opinion".[60] Lohia, however, does not want to reject negative peace outright. Being a practical man, Lohia wants the third camp to use the period of negative peace "for removing the causes of war; otherwise, it is an interval during which the combatants arm themselves for a grimmer struggle". Lohia further wants the non-aligned nations "to strive for both types of peace, for a world order in which peace inheres as well as for correcting excesses of the existing semblance of order".[61] He regrets that instead of adopting confrontationanist attitude with the two power blocs, they accept from them economic or military aid. The foreign aid actually ties up Asian people with one or the other of the conformist systems, therefore, the foreign aid must be rejected summarily. Nevertheless, Lohia is not against foreign aid totally. He welcomes economic aid in the form of investment, bearing interests and reasonable profit. This aid must be used to build true socialism at home. It should not distract attention from the basic task of planning internal resources. Lohia expects that "to be useful foreign aid must be treated as a solvent to that crisis in human civilization...."[62] Being purist in his attitude towards the ideal of world order, Lohia wishes that the foreign aid be given with a view to raising minimum defeat standard of living to every person on the early. It should be given as a duty and not as obligation, by economically powerful nations. Lohia writes, "the foreign aid must therefore be as plentiful as are the war budgets. When the immediate provision of a minimum and ultimately a decent standard of living to every person on earth becomes the duty of all citizens and states, foreign aid will in reality become an instrument of the new order".[63]

Thus, Lohia is in favour of accepting foreign aid selectively which helps building the world order based on equality and justice.

According to Lohia, all the factors which come in the way to the creation of world order can be removed provided the nations of the world have determination to do so. Lohia overemphasizes the role of will power in the creation of new world order. The will power will discard the ideologies of communism and capitalism and will create the ideology of 'socialism' for the future world order. In order to create a new world order based on the ideology of socialism, Lohia suggests institutional arrangement.

New Institutions for Transformation

In order to create a new world civilization based on the principle of "total efficiency" in respect of the whole of mankind as well as the individual, Lohia suggests creating two new institutions - World Government and the World Development Authority.

World Government : Parliament of Man, Not Nations

According to Lohia, the World Government will be consisting of a world parliament. In order to give justice to the small nations of the world in their representation to the World Parliament, Lohia puts forward two solutions:

a. The World Parliament may consist of two houses: in the upper house each nation should be accorded equal representation regardless of its population; and
b. In a single house of World Parliament, the constituencies may be so bifurcated as to achieve adult franchise along with regional weightage.[64]

The world government will not be created unless the nations are ready to surrender their sovereignty and it is doubtful whether nations will ever be ready to surrender their sovereignty totally. Hence, Lohia suggests that nations should surrender that aspect of sovereignty which relates to peace and war. Lohia advocates to elect the world parliament on the basis of adult franchise as it will create a direct link between individual and the world state. Lohia writes, "In order to achieves universality and equality, the only known method available is that of adult franchise".[65]

Lohia is convinced that the method of adult franchise will help to create a world public opinion through elections. It will undermine the paradigm of nation-state. Secondly, it will call into question the reality of existing power politics based on inequality and injustice. Thirdly, it will evolve a world political process which is essential to create a world institution. Moreover, it will help creating relations based on man to man than on nation to nation.

Powers of World Parliament

Lohia wants to restrict powers of the world parliament to only two subjects, i.e., right to impose peace and to help in reconstruction.

In order to implement peace, Lohia suggests a principle of 'collective security' to be incorporated in the World Government. The system of collective security can be implemented with the establishment of international armed forces. Side by side, the world parliament must try to make nations to accept the principle of progressive disarmament of nations. The progressive disarmament will correct the excesses of the existing semblance of order.

For economic reconstruction of the world order, Lohia suggests establishment of the World Development Authority. This authority must initiate some schemes of reconstruction of world economy to improve agriculture or industries. As far as its source of income is concerned, Lohia suggests that it may "Organize a pool of resources in capital and skill from each nation according to its needs".[66] He also suggests an alternative scheme if this scheme is found to be too vague. He writes, "should this formula be found to be too vague, a fixed percentage of the war budget may go into this pool".[67]

Lohia is hopeful that this type of parliament will come into existence. It will be not only an improvement upon the UNO but will go beyond that, he praises such a parliament, "As such an organization starts coming into being, it will inevitably tend to become a better repository for the conscience of mankind instead of being a clearing house of international intrigue and will therefore, have greater moral authority over nations and will also exercise increasing powers such as those of world force or a world development authority".[68]

Being a realist, Lohia knows that it will be very difficult to give birth to such an organization, as nations and governments will not be ready to surrender their authority. In order to make this possible, the people will have to make sacrifices. Lohia says, "It will be achieved when it becomes a passionate need of the suffering millions".[69]

People must be made aware of the need for the world parliament. In order to make people aware and to create the world public opinion in favour of a world parliament, Lohia dreams of a political party within nations having long term programme to create such an institution.

Lohia thinks that mankind requires political parties which can make a hundred year or a fifty year programme of international policy. It is because, in Lohia's world, "The World is basically diseased in its international relationships. Its foundations have rotted. New foundations have to be laid".[70] At present no political party anywhere takes up any bold policy on international relations. Lohia regrets that on the contrary, all political parties have chosen to become drum beaters of their native governments. They are afraid to think radically. They fear that the radical policy will not fetch votes to them. They also fear that they may not be able to practice in office radicalism in office that they profess. These two fears are interrelated. Insisting upon his idea Lohia writes, "A government or a foreign office may not be able to take up this position openly and aggressively. But political parties, whose function it is to change men's minds and behaviour, are obligated to take up such position".[71]

Lohia was thus thoroughly dissatisfied with the existing international order of his time, as it was characterized by the existence of dominant powers. Dominant powers did not work for the united world (one world), but they produce an order which caused civil wars among many nations, generated poverty world wide and gave birth to the situation of war (as it is that period was characterized by (Cold War). That order further causes inequality among nations and also gross inequality within the nations. The Cold War politics generated an order which .was status-quoist. It functioned in the interests of the super powers. In Lohia's view, what was needed was restructuring of that order. In order to restructure the existing order, he suggested two pronged strategy - first the creation of the third camp consisted of the non-aligned nations and empowering of the United Nations Organizations.

Secondly, in order to do away with the existing order and to create a new order he suggested an another strategy to go beyond the existing order, dominated by the nation-states actors. Lohia, like Kant, opted for a new society composed of men and not sovereign states. The principle of "total efficiency" (the total development of individual's personality) should be the guiding axiom for reorganizing human society. Thus for

Lohia the general good is "total efficiency" of an individual and nothing less than that. In other words, a just and permanently peaceful global society can not be created unless each individual becomes capable to develop his personality fully.

To sum up Lohia's conception one has to understand that, he interprets the notion of the world civilization in terms of political ideologies. Unlike Gandhi, he believes that the present civilization based on science and technology is capable of producing just and equitable global order and peace, but the main stumbling bloc is the structure of the nation-state system. The nation-states are sharply divided and they subscribe to the incompatible ideologies of communism and capitalism. These ideologies are the product of the new civilization. Hence, the fragmented nation-states prefers to use the forces of science and technology for raising standard of living of their (people) nation at the cost of other people.

Lohia believes that, in the name of ideologies, they want to perpetuate the existing order composed of the nation-states. This order is based on militarism, centralization of power, rationalization in production and exploitation of all resources for the development of their own people. He is convinced that both the blocs are not interested in changing international order which works in their favour. They are least interested in creating a world order based on justice. Lohia perceives that their methods have changed, but their aims have remained the same. The methods they employ now are economic enslavement of the underdeveloped countries by means of loans and military aid.

In order to combat the activities of the two blocs, Lohia works out a thesis of the Third Camp in world affairs. The Third camp comprising of the newly independent states of Asia, Africa and Latin America should denounce militarism and expansionist policy of these blocs. Lohia visualizes that only the effective opinion of a third camp will influence and compel the two warring camps to pursue a policy of peace and disarmament and non-aggression in respect of weak and underdeveloped countries of the world. What Lohia seems to suggest to the third world countries is selective non-cooperation with the dominant power. It seems what Lohia has in mind is that this type of non-cooperation will weaken the nation-state system.

In the realm of ideology, Lohia propagates the ideology of socialism based on the premise of universal brotherhood. He is faithful that powerful ideology of socialism will be combating against the outdated ideologies of communism and capitalism. The ideology and capitalism.

The ideology of socialism incorporates Gandhian ideals and methods of civil disobedience. It seems Lohia seeks for the application and operationalizatin of Gandhian model of survodaya at international level in order to create a society of mankind at world level.

What Lohia suggests is that, the existing seemingly emancipative ideologies of communism and capitalism are defective. Moreover, the instruments (Nation-State System) through which ideologies are implemented is equally defective. In order to rectify these defects, Lohia suggests to replicate the Gandhian model at the international level to server as competent alternative for achieving world peace.

Lohia's writings on international relations have historical orientation and exhibit insight into the power relations in the contemporary world. He advocates socialist (New Socialism) aspirations for world order based on the principle of international brotherhood. But at the same time he views recent history as a struggle for supremacy between nations, continents and civilizations in which Europe has always been the oppressor.

In the writings of Lohia, one is struck with his exposition of the synthesis of oriental thinking as well as modern conflicts between the two worlds of communism and capitalism (democratic individualism). According to him, the conflict in the international society is the conflict of civilization. The modern European civilization does not help developing human personality. Hence his central thesis is regarding how to achieve total efficiency and how to relate it to development of human personality through the evolution of a new world civilization. Lohia envisages a world of total efficiency. He aims at evolving a world culture of such magnitude based on the principle of total efficiency.

The two existing blocks are struggling for the attainment of maximum efficiency for their own people by developing national output and pushing up standard of living within national boundaries in two different ways. According to Lohia, they come in the way of creating a just world order. Just world order can be created by producing a stateless society. The communism the capitalism may, however, claim to usher ultimately an era of stateless society, they have, in fact, maintained a status-quo to safeguard their status and interests.

In order to revise the unjust status-quo, Lohia suggests to replicate the Gandhian model of 'satyagraha', a struggle insisting on truth, at the international level by coordinating peace movements occurring differently in countries of the world under the leadership of the third camp mainly comprised of the non-aligned nations. Sable order and just peace can be created at the global level provided we create a stateless international society and classless societies at national levels composed of human beings, with the help of the ideology of socialism.

NOTES AND REFERENCES

1. *Lohia, Ram Manohar,* Notes and Comments, *Vol. II, Prakashan Vighag, Hyderabad, 1072,* p. 85.
2. *Lohia, Ram Manohar,* Wheel of History, *Prakashan Vibhag, Hyderabad, 1955, reprinted 1974. The entire book reflects his philosophy of history.*
3. See No. 1, Vol. II, p. 85.
4. *Gupta, R.C.,* The Great Political Thinkers, *East and West, Agra, 1974, p. 188.*
5. *Mehrotra, N.C.,* Lohia : A Study, *Atma Ram and Sons, Delhi, 1978, pp. 208-10.*
6. *Lohia, Ram Manohar,* Will to Power and Other Writings, *Navhind Publication, Hyderabad, 1956, p. 71.*
7. See No. 1, Vol. I, Chapter 6, pp. 83-85.
8. Ibid., pp..2-5.
9. Ibid., pp. 338-339.
10. *Lohia, Ram Manohar,* Will to Power, *p. 73.*
11. Ibid.
12. See No. 4, pp. 187-95.
13. Ibid., pp. 187-188.
14. *Lohia, Ram Manohar,* The Driving Forces of History : An Analysis, *Janata, Vol. 7, No. 1, July 20, 1952, p. 2.*
15. See No. 10, pp. 79-83.
16. Ibid.
17. See No. 5, p. 205.
18. See No. 10, p. 78.
19. *Lohia, Ram Manohar,* The Meaning of Equality in Mankind, *No. 4, Nov. 1956,* pp. 366-380.
20. See No. 4, p. 190.
21. See No. 19.
22. Ibid.
23. Ibid.
24. See No. 1, Vol. II, No. 6, pp. 83-89.
25. See No. 5, Chapter 6, p. 200. In 1940, *Lohia wrote a letter to Gandhiji formulated the four point programme for world peace which Gandhiji published in* Harijan, Jan, 1, 1940.

26. *Lohia, Ram Manohar,* Marx, Gandhi and Socialism, *See Preface, Navhind, Hyderabad, 1963 (First Publsihed) (The Second Edition in 1978).*
27. See No. 5, p. 201.
28. See No. 6, pp. 71-7.
29. Ibid.
30. See No. 1, Vol. II, No. 23, pp. 134-141.
31. See No. 5, pp. 205-209. Also see, Lohia, "Third Force Alone Can Avert War" in Janata, Vol. 5, No. 48, December 17, 1950, pp. 506, and 14; and Janata, vol. 6, No. 47, December 23, 1951, pp. 6-7. Also refer "Third Camp in World Affairs", Madhu Limye, `for the Socialist Party', National House, Bombay.
32. Ibid.
33. Ibid.
34. See No. 6, p. 78.
35. *Lohia, Ram Manohar,* Non-Alignment, *Vol. II, p. 134.*
36. See No. 31.
37. See No. 5, pp. 205-208.
38. Ibid., p. 208.
39. Ibid.
40. Ibid.
41. Ibid., p. 220.
42. Ibid., p. 220.
43. See No. 6, p. 80.
44. Ibid., pp. 80-81.
45. Ibid., p. 80.
46. Ibid.
47. Ibid., p. 71.
48. Ibid., p. 71.
49. Ibid.
50. See No. 2.
51. Ibid.
52. Ibid.
53. Ibid.
54. Ibid.
55. Ibid.
56. Ibid.
57. See No. 6, p. 74.
58. See No. 5, pp. 205-208.
59. See No. 6, p. 75.

60. Ibid.
61. See No. 5, pp. 205-208.
62. See No. 1, Vol. II.
63. Ibid.
64. See No. 5, p. 222. 65. Ibid.
66. Ibid.
67. Ibid., pp. 222-23.
68. Ibid., p. 223.
69. Ibid.
70. See No. 5, p. 223 and also No. 6, pp. 76-77.
71. See No. 1, Vol. I, No. 6, p. 87.

Chapter 5

CONCLUSION

The concluding chapter is divided into four parts in order to present and relate the ideas of the classical theorists like. Thomas Hobbes (1588-1679), Immanuel Kant (1724-1804) and Hugo Grotius (1583-1679) with those of Mohandas Gandhi (1869-1948), Jawaharlal Nehru (1889-1964) and Ram Manohar Lohia (1910-1967) in a systematic way.

The first part rationalises as to how Gandhi, Nehru and Lohia articulate their ideas on the problematique of international order and world peace against the backdrop of the similar problematique as responded by the three western thinkers viz. Hobbes, Kant and Grotius —almost three hundred years ago. These three thinkers provided conceptual categories which facilitate comparison and help in defining the paradigms of international relations political theory.

The second part conceptualizes views of Indian thinkers and their perception on the notion of international society, its nature, its functioning and (dis)organizing principles.

The third part conceptualizes the ideas of Gandhi, Nehru and Lohia on the (dis)order in international society and their conception on international society which further shape following sub-categories; what is order; what are the institutions which maintain it; whether it is progressive or regressive; whether they want to maintain that order or want to improve and transcend it; and their strategy of improvement (or transformation).

The fourth part conceptualizes their ideas in terms of new values, which they suggest in order to reorganize international society. This is a unique contribution of the Indian Peace Studies to the area of peace research in problematique of global order and peace, not attended by the Indian scholars for want of disparateness of ideas of Gandhi, Nehru and Lohia.

In order to have a glance on the span of thinking from Hobbes to Lohia on such a vital problematique, an appendix is attached which furnishes in a tabular form a comprehensive enclosed overview and a comparative analysis of all the thinkers at the end of the chapter.

This study focuses on global order and peace mainly because it is a problem of all times pestering and hammering the human mind, and the grim reality of today is that there is no central agency at the global level to ensure peace and order as we find within the national societies of nation-states.

The main dichotomy between the national and international society is characterized by the concept of 'civil society' and 'anarchy' respectively. The basic pursuance of the national (domestic) society is to achieve "good life" and that of the international society is "the survival of a state". Hence the problem arises who creates 'order' in an anarchical society and 'how' it is maintained so that the war can be prevented and peace can be preserved. In order words, the fundamental focus is to find out how the international anarchy is conceived by Gandhi, Nehru and Lohia as to how it is managed and how it ought to be managed in the interest of permanent peace. The focus is how to create order in the absence of world government so that anarchical society can be transformed into a civil society.

As mentioned in the introduction, the main purpose of this study is to conceptualize idea of Indian thinkers, Gandhi, Nehru and Lohia around this problematique by addressing the most fundamental theoretical question of the discipline of international relations: what do they mean by international society?

I

Comparative Categories

In this part, the conceptions of Thomas Hobbes, Immanuel Kant, Hugo Grotius, Mohandas Gandhi, Jawaharlal Nehru and Ram Manohar Lohia are poured into four categories with a view to juxtaposing their conceptions of international society. Following the classical tradition of theorizing these categories are put in three sub-sections. First, the causes of war and conditions of peace and order, second, the identification of essential actors of the international society. (The classical theoretical tradition considers 'the sovereign states' as the essential actors or unit of analysis) and the third and formulation of their world view. The dominant image of the world in classical tradition is a system of sovereign states characterized by 'international anarchy'.

I. The Causes of War and Conditions of Peace

Thomas Hobbes

Hobbes locates the causes of war in human nature. Human beings fight for greed, pride and covetousness. In Hobbes views, the international society is in a state of nature, i.e., in a pre-contractual stage. This implies chaos and disorder. Lack of order is associated with the situation of state of war. Nevertheless, for Hobbes a posture of war is a permanent and typical characteristic of international politics. He however, neither proposes a plan for perpetual peace nor evolve any strategy for eliminating the phenomena of war from international relations. But he does provokes us to think of an alternative mode of conflict management at international level.

Immanuel Kant

Kant, like Hobbes, defines this essential problematique in terms of war and conditions of peace and order. He also locates causes of war in human nature. Lust for power, glory and wealth are the main causes of war. Kant maintains that human nature can be improved by education. The human mind needs to be constantly hammered and reminded of higher and finer values. In this way he can be led away from objects which creep into his nature eventually leading to war. Kant is of the opinion that wars are basically the blunders committed by princes. If people are given power to declare war, they will be reluctant to do so for several reasons.

His ultimate goal is to create a global community of individuals. Kant holds that republic nations only can be assigned membership of his confederation. They will the, feel secured, not any supernatural authority imposed on them, but by mutual recognition, among the confederate states, of their rights and duties vis-a-vis other national. Kant assumes that this sort of individual-to-individual contact between states would produce pacific relations between states which would respect rule of law at home and abroad. Thus, gradually a global civil society will emerge.

Hugo Grotius

Grotius also defines the essential problematique every much in terms of the phenomena of war and conditions of peace and order. However, he does not provide an inquiry into causes of war. He is concerned more with imposing limits on the recourse to and the conduct of war. In fact, Grotius begins with the assumption that war is inevitable and indeed is in perfect accord with the first principle of nature, for the aim of war is the preservation of life and limb (of the sovereign state in the society of states). Nevertheless, he distinguishes between just and unjust wars positing that the law of nations sanctions only such wars which are fought to assert or defend the community or the societal rights. Thus Grotius believes that war may occur but it should be subjected to legal and moral regulation both as to the cause, for which it is fought and the way in which it is fought. Grotius understands the phenomena of war not just a deviation, but a reflection of incompleteness and inadequacies of the norms prescribed to provide a good deal of order in international society.

The Grotian tradition does not believe in Hobbessian assertion, "the war of all against all", but presumes sovereign states as "the family of nations". Grotius further presumes that the sovereign states themselves are interested in preserving order. It is evident in their diplomatic treaty and other institutions. Grotius is convinced that the totality of international relations is subject to the rule of law. Thus, he provides a notion of natural law as normative framework for the nation-states to behave like a society and not merely as a system.

Gandhi

Gandhi like Hobbes, Kant and Grotius defines the essential problematique in terms of war and conditions of peace, stability and order. He provides an indepth analysis of the causes of war and discusses the reasons for the break down of international order. Gandhi, like Kant locates the basic causes of war in human nature. He blames the unrighteousness on the part of the national leaders and their faith in violence to fulfill their ambitions. Lust for power and wealth, in Gandhi's views, result into exploitation and desire to dominate others in this way human nature is the root cause of outbreak of war. Besides human nature, he also blames injustice in-built within the nation-state system. In order to turn international nation-state system into international society, the ordering units (nation-states) must function harmoniously. This harmony can be created provided 'order' is created on the principle of 'natural law' and maintained through some value-system, viz. non-violence and justice.

Nevertheless, Gandhi presumes that some sort of order prevails in relations between nation-states. In Gandhi's view it is precarious and inadequate. Thus Gandhi's orientation of international order is mainly connected with the problem of disequilibrium among nations. He calls for the elimination of all forms of violence which create disequilibrium, both overtly and covertly at all levels of human life. Thus, Gandhi's conception of order refers to natural harmony without distortion. His conception of order also refers to the necessity of meshing various parts in such a way that they interact without distortion. Moreover, Gandhi also wants that it should reflect some idea of justice, otherwise it will not last for ever. Gandhi's conception of order, in short, is connected with the idea of a particular equilibrium — international or human. Harmony between the units of international society (between nation-states) can preserve peace.

Nehru

Nehru, blames the human nature basically for outbreak of war. he specifically blames lust for power, greed and self-interest breading in one's nature. But he goes one step further to point out that psychological affliction of fear is the chief cause of war. In Nehru's views, the psychosis of fear affects men's thinking. It is fear that promotes hatred of nation against another.

Along with psychological factors, Nehru blames political and economic factors too for outbreak of war.

Nehru was convinced that peace does not prevail in international society because, the nation-states adopt wrong means to preserve peace, such as, the devises of alliances and counter alliances, the balance of power, deterrent etc. Moreover, they prepare for war in order to preserve peace. He appeals that good means must be employed for good ends.

Lohia

Unlike his processors — Hobbes, Grotius, Kant, Gandhi and Nehru, Lohia does not address the causes of war and the problem of security directly. He therefore, does not give a forthright answer to the problematique. To him the problematique of war and peace are the problem of reorganization of entire human society. The solutions which he suggests at two levels are also related to restructuring international order at the international societal level composed of nation-states as well as reorganizing human society at global level.

He, however, does not analyze the problematique of war in terms of human psychology. He rather looks at the phenomena of war as a product of the unjust order created by the international society composed of nation-states.

Lohia's concerns are mainly two: First, concentration of powers in the hands of a few nations, chiefly European at the international level. Second, many in the human society are denied the opportunity to realize their inner potential. In order to create a just society, Lohia advocates decentralization of power at all levels so that a genuine equality amongst the nations and individuals can be maintained and the true liberty can be experienced by all. If it is done, atmosphere will be created in which every individual will be able to realize his inner potential fully and it is Lohia's ideal that society ought to be is composed of happy men.

II. The Unit of Analysis or The Essential Actors

To the classical thinkers Hobbes, Kant and Grotius, the main unit of analysis of sovereign states, states and system of states, the essential actors and their behaviour remain the central focus of the study of international politics. The problem and proposed remedies are discussed in terms of actions of states within the context of a European state system. Only sovereign states are the members of the society. Eighteenth century thinkers acknowledged neither the existence nor importance of non-state actors, as they are understood today.

Gandhi, Nehru and Lohia too, define the essential problematique in terms of sovereign states and the system of states. They also 'consider sovereign states as the only members of the society. The status of nation-states in the new context. During the time of classical lived the society of states was limited to Europe. That tradition continued even in the time of Gandhi, Nehru and Lohia. Hence, the three of them want that the society of states be expanded to Asia and Africa.

One distinct difference is that Gandhi, Nehru and Lohia refer to the League of Nations and the United Nations Organization as non-state actos. Lohia goes one step further to suggest political processes should be managed at international level.

III. Images of the World or World View

Thomas Hobbes, Kant and Grotius speak of the European system, and not of a global system as it exists today. They considered the rest of the world (Africa-Asia) as uncivilized (savages). The notion of independent states operating within some sort of order was common to thinkers of the classical tradition. However, these three of them disagreed regarding the degree of order and "society" among the states remained and still continues, to be the issue of the debate. So the key question dividing them is the degree of order, and the presence or absence of the quality of a "society" of states. One thing needs to be noted that although all three presume an anarchical nature of the existing international society to start with, Grotius, does not admit it openly nor does he talk about the central government at the global level.

The dominant presumptions of Gandhi, Nehru and Lohia are the same that international politics is monopolized by the great power in the absence of a world government. Ironically, Gandhi, Nehru and Lohia dubbed the great powers as uncivilized and savages without overtly using there words because they dominated the rest of the world for their selfish interest. They do not respect human dignity and perpetuate injustice on them with the help of armaments and misinterpreting 'notion of nationalism'. They too agree with the existence of 'anarchy' at international level. But they blame the dominant power to perpetuate anarchy as it functions in their interest. They are thoroughly dissatisfied with the 'order' created and controlled by the dominant powers. Hence, all of them suggest change in the status-quo, and never speak in terms of system maintenance as it is. But they call for system improvement. They even go further and write extensively about transcending the nation-states system. Al of them, in final analysis opt for not only classless but even stateless society mainly organized around the notion of 'human dignity'.

II

The Notion of International Society : Anarchical and Hgemonial

Gandhi, Nehru and Lohia (intituvely) perceived that the international society is mainly composed of nation-states in which the people's welfare is not given due attention. They resent the neglect of the welfare of the mankind. Hence all of them focus upon the improvement in the functioning of the nation-state system. Their first priority, therefore, is improvement and systemic changes in the system, rather than transformation of the system. Nevertheless, they do suggest strategies for the system transformation. So that the system can, function in the interest of humanity and the dominating interests of nation-states considering survival their priority may be curbed and minimized in their influence. They expressed their profound dissatisfaction that in international relations and in its functioning people (individuals) have been neglected as if they do not matter.

Three of them also understand anarchical nature of international society and in the absence of the central authority, the great powers manage the political affairs of the world in their own interest at the cost of others. In Gandhi's views, it is not the entire nation but a small group of the powerful people who control the destiny of mankind. This dominant group neglect the majority of the people residing even within their own states, and develop a vested interest in perpetuating their hold on the nation as it helps them to control the world at large. Hence, in order to perpetuate their hold on the national society, they exploit the people's feeling of nationalism. They misinterpret nationalism and, thus, misguide the masses who are ignorant of international relations. This group of people create an anarchy within the nation, which is further reflected in the international society. Gandhi suggests that all the human beings are bound by the invisible principle of national law. It is principle of harmony and mutual interdependence of all elements on the globe. Gandhi wants us to be conscious about it as it is the truth. Gandhi wants, therefore, the nation-state system to function according to the principle of truth so that stable global order and a genuine peace can be created for every one on the earth.

Nehru and Lohia on the other hand, blame the nation-state system for the anarchical nature of the international society. They believe that the functioning of the system is monopolized by a few nations. They dominate the rest of the world and become prosperous at the cost of the other nations. It happens because the decision-making at the international level, rests with those few. Therefore, Nehru wants that international society should be democratized. Being a liberal thinker, he does not advocate the confrontationist approach between the core powers and the peripheral powers. He opts for an institutional approach. He wants that the final decision-making power should be shifted from the great powers to the United Nations organization. He wants other nations to adopt a persuasive and peaceful approach.

In contrast to Nehru, Lohia advocates the confrontationist approach by the emergence of the Third Camp (against the Eastern USSR and the Western Camp) equally powerful, militarily and otherwise. Lohia believes that the grant powers will listen to the peripheral powers, provided the third camp learns to talk to them on equal footings. If the near parity is created between the haves and the haves- not the international society will move in the direction of democratization.

However, all of the — Gandhi, Nehru and Lohia — condemn the great powers for mismanagement of the global political life and their methods of exploiting the anarchical nature of society for their own advantage.

III

Meaning, Nature and Maintenance of (Dis)Order and the Methods to Improve Or Transcend It

Gandhi, Nehru and Lohia believe that nation-states definitely create order as they are active units of the system. No one of them, therefore wish to do away with nation-state system. Nevertheless, they suggest different strategies to improve and transcend it. They are of the view that in the absence of the central authority at the global level, the order is maintained mainly by the 'violent means'. They disapprove of it, and suggest different ways of doing away with system of armaments, arms race and weapon culture. The nation-states have immense faith in (physical) "force" (or threat to use force) to keep order in international society. Gandhi, Nehru and Lohia want nation-states to generate moral strength from within than in the means of destruction. They warn them against indiscriminate use of violence in a thermo-nuclear age lest they will destroy themselves and bring total destruction of the earth. Weapons which are sheer means of destruction - are neutral in terms of values and ethical standards - it is man who uses them has to make value judgment in this regard.

Nehru, being a serious follower of history, did realise that the time had come to take the initiative in preventing the cycle of balance of power. Balance of power despite being responsible for the two world wars - perpetuates as the sole means of resolving conflicts and maintenances of order. If the sovereign state system is to be restored to its genuine objective (regulating inter-state relations without taking recourse to weapons or war), then the Balance of power needs to be replaced by more civilized ways of interaction.

Gandhi and Nehru specifically blame human nature for outbreak of war. Gandhi appeals for introspection, while Nehru pleads to confine politics within the bounds of the United Nations organization. Nehru thinks that, at least, the international institution (like UNO) will be able to institutionalize the game of power politics as the great powers will check-mate each other even through the veto-power and war will not break out. For Nehru though the Gandhian scheme of peace which rested on non-violent means was ideal - the international environment was not conducive for such an experiment and therefore it was necessary to entrust the great powers with sense of responsibility under the UN armed with the Veto power. Lohia holds a different view that the Great Powers, mainly European, are interested in perpetuating unjust order in international society. As the present order functions in their interest, they will never give it up. He insists that they should be forced to change the order. Unless the third world countries reciprocate the great powers - policies in the same measure that will continue to dictate and dominate. He pleads for the unity of the non-aligned countries which could develop equally powerful front against the two great powers the USA and the

USSR. It will create a symmetrical situation vis-a-vis the great powers. They, then, will be forced to negotiate with the peripheral powers on the principle of equality. The great powers will also be compelled to democratize the international order and, as a result, just international society will emerge.

Thus, Lohia opts for a 'power approach', against Nehru's 'institutional approach', and Gandhi's moralistic approach. The trio of Gandhi, Nehru and Lohia collectively resent ideologies of imperialism, colonialism, capitalism and communism which exploit the order in international society. Apart from the merits or demerits of these ideologies, they condemn them as great powers use them for perpetuating their hold on the nation-state system. In the same fashion, they condemned peace treaties, and the international institutions, (the League of the UNO), which the great powers conceived in the name of creating a new world order. Gandhi, Nehru and Lohia expose their game to perpetuate their dominance on the system and suggest modification, especially in the structure of the UNO.

Gandhi, Nehru and Lohia perceives that the existing order is a viable alternative methods of improving as well as transcending the nation-states system.

Strategy of Improving the functioning of the System

Gandhi, Nehru and Lohia further perceived the nation-state system as conducive neither to the attainment of global peace and justice nor to the fulfillment of social, economic, political aspirations of newly decolonized states. Consequently, they devote a considerable amount of effort to conceive reforms or to suggest alternative to the nation-state system.

Several similarities can be noticed in their conceptualization of the changes required in the nation-state system. Each of them makes his contribution indicating his individual, social and cultural predilections. All three advocate expansion of the nation-state system which was confined to Western Europe. In fact throughout their lives they worked and fought for decolonization, as well for asserting a place at the UNO as its member. If it is done, the principle of equality within the committee of nations should be accepted. In that case, justice would prevail within the nation-state system. They also suggest and strongly plead for total disarmament as the arm-race would not allow nation-state system to function in the interest of all. It is operating in a way breeds injustice and inequality.Moreover they wanted that cooperation should be basis of its functioning.

In order to transcend the system, Gandhi emphasise an individual approach while Nehru and Lohia opt for 'institutional' approach. Gandhi does not have faith in the League of the UNO as it reflected only the power reality. Gandhi wants the two processes the decentralization of power and resocialization of man - be operationalize simultaneously, to transcend the system. Primarily, Nehru and Lohia advocate the political approach to peace. They seek peace through 'states' and other institutions. They suggest either improvement in their functioning or creation of alternative institutions, national or international. By suggesting the creation of other institutions, (World Parliament, World Economic Development Council, etc.) they think that they would create an alternative power structure, as these institutions would undermine the role the state as a powerful institution. Nehru-Lohia differ from Gandhi in their approach as they suggest a quite opposite framework for transforming the system. However, they remarkably agree to each other in aims and objectives of creating a just and global order and peace.

India's Contribution to Peace-Studies in Term of New Values

Being a prophet of peace, Gandhi operates at two levels; individual as well as societal. At individual level, he blames a small group of people which operates at the national level for the decision-making. The same group is responsible for malfunctioning of the international society. He appeals to them to give up their greed and lust for power. He wants them to take out 'fear' from their heart, put an end to violence and keep themselves and their nations free. Gandhi urges them to have more faith in themselves than in a system of armament, as weapon can not generate peace. Peace can be generated by a man with confidence in himself.

Thus, Gandhi goes one step further than Immanuel Kant to suggest the creation of Pacific Union (confederation) of the sovereign states.

Nehru's entire efforts are directed to avoid the outbreak of the Third World War. Being a practicing politician, he suggests norms called, "Panchsheel" so that a deadly game of politics may be regulated and war can atleast be postponed, if not avoided altogether.

Nehru's time was the time of the Cold War politics. It would have led to the Third World War. He strongly preached everywhere and practiced, wherever possible, the value of cooperation among the nation-states. He strived for replacement of the politics of confrontationist by the politics of cooperation.

Lohia, being an agitationalist politician, suggests to create unity among the deprived powers and to cultivate political will to confront the big powers. He wants the nonaligned nations to acquire more and more strength to confront their big brothers so that they can yield to the demand of the peripheral powers.

Contribution of Lohia lies in his suggestion of total reorganization of human society based on the principle of 'total efficiency' and not on that of 'maximum efficiency'. In other words, he strongly advocates that the society should be so organized that every individual can develop his/her personality fully without any hitch or hindrance.

The Indian Peace Studies bring out the inadequacies of the nature of the international society as well as the mismanagement of international order. The trio of Gandhi, Nehru and Lohia strongly advocate the reorganization of the existing human society based on the organizing principles of rationality, cooperation and the dignity of the human being.

However idealistic their approach to peace may appear, the fact remains that the ultimate triumph of what constitutes and distinguishes human being from other animal must come to play its role. Gandhi, Nehru and Lohia, in their own way, somewhat unconsciously, come very close to what Hobbes, Kant and Grotius had perceived as the eternal clash within the realm of physical and mental world and how he has been struggling to liberate himself from the clutches of baser instinct. Gandhi, Nehru and Lohia take that struggle further with a firm conviction to restore natural humanness to human being by suggesting ways and means of shunning the impact of the negative forces. Thus, this study makes a modest attempt to reconcile the great ideas, irrespective of their sources and vindicates that 'the universal man' exists and scholars have to continue to locate him in their own respective milieu. This has been the motivating force behind this study.

BIBLIOGRAPHY

On the theory of International Politics, the British Committee was set up in England comprising of mainly scholars and practioners which for some twenty five years (1959-84) met under the chairmanship first of Herbert Butterfield, then of Martin Wight, then of Adam Watson and lastly of Hedley Bull. They discussed the theoretical problematique in depth and presented many studied papers. The main ideas of those papers subsequently published in seven books. The ideas expressed in these books. The ideas expressed in these books from the basis of my study on Gandhi, Nehru and Lohia. They arc listed here :

1. Bull, H. and Watson, A., (ed.), *The Expansion of International Society*, Oxford University Press, Oxford, 1984.
2. Bull, H., *The Anarchical Society*, Macmillan, London and Golumbia University Press, New York.
3. Butterfield, H., *The Whig Interpretation of History*, Bell, London, 1951.
4. Butterfield, H., "The Balance of Power", in *The Dictionary of the History of Ideas*, Scribners, New York, 1973.
5. Butterfield, H., and Wight, M. (eds.) *Diplomatic Investigations,* Allen and Unwin, London, 1966. It contains two seminal essays: Wight on "Why is there no International Theory?" and Butterfield on the "Balance of Power".
6. Wight, M., (with introduction by H. Bull) *Systems of States,* Leicester University Press, Leicester, 1977.
7. Adam Watson, *The Evolution of International Society : A comparatie Historical Analysis,* Routledge, London, 1992.

Alan, James, (ed.), *The Bases of International Order* (Eassays in Honour of C.A.W. Manning), London, Oxford University Press. See especially essays by Martin Wight, "The Balance of Power and International Order and by Michael Banks, Charless Manning, "The Concept of Order and Contemporary International Theory" and also by F.S. Northedge, "Order and Change in International Society".

Aron, R., *Peace and War : A Theory of International Relations*, Anchor Press, New York, 1973.

Beitz, C.R., *Political Theory and International Relations*, N.J. University Press, Princeton, 1979.

Brown, Lester, "World Without Borders, "Random House, New York, 1972.

Donelan, M. (ed.) *The Reason of States*, Allen and Unwin, London, 1978.

Gallie, W.B., *Philosophers of Peace and War*, Kant, Clausewitz, Marx, Engles and Tolstoy, cambridge University Press, Cambridge, 1978.

Galtung, Johan, *The True World : A Transnational Perspective*, The Free Press, New York, 1980.

Hinsley, F.H., *Power and the Pursuit of Peace*, Cambridge University Press, Cambridge (ntroduction of this book is must to read), 1963; and *Nationalism and the International System*, New York, 1973. Refer especially Chapter 4.

Holsti, K.J., *The Dividing Discipline : Hegemony and Diversity in International Theory*, Allen and Unwin, Boston, 1985.

Kennedy, P. *The Rise and Fall of the Great Powers : Economic Change and Military Conflict From 1500 to 2000*, Random House, New York, 1987.

Kenneth, Thomson, *Masters of International Thought : Major Twentieth Century Theorists and the World Crisis*, Laussiana State University Press, 1959.

Michael, Banks and Martin Shaw, *State and Society in International Relations*, Harvester Wheatsheaf in New York, London, Toronto, Sydney, Tokyo and Singapore, 1991.

Morgenthau, H., *Politica Among Nations*, New York, 1978.

Morse, E., *Modernization and Transformation of International Relations*, Free Press, New York, 1976 (Refer Chapter 2 on Westphalia settlement).

Parkinson, F., *The Philosophy of International Relations : A Study in the History of Thought*, Sage Publication, London, 1970.

Waltz, Kenneth, *Man, the State and War*, Columbia University Press, New York, 1954.

THOMAS HOBBES

Airakainen, and Bertman, Martin A. (ed.), *Hobbes : War Among Nations*, U.S.A. 1989.

Baumgold (Deborah), *Hobbes's Political Theory*, Cambridge University, Press, 1988.

Brown, K.C., (ed.), *Hobbes Studies*, Basil Blackwell, Oxford, 1965.

Hedley, Bull, "Hobbes and the International Anarchy", in Mukherjee and Ramswami (ed.), *Great Western Thinkers.*

Hiram, Caton, *On the Basis of Hobbes Political Philosophy.*

Leo, Strauss, *On the Sprit of Hobbes Political Philosophy.*

Macopherson, C.B., "Hobbes : Analysts of Power and Peace", n Subrata Mukherjee and Sushila Ramswami (ed.), *Great Western Political Thinkers,* Vol. 4, Deep and Deep, New Delhi, 1993. See introduction to the volume by Macpherson is recommended.

Mark, Grae, *Hobbes and His Audience : The Dynamics of Theorizing.*

Murry, Forsyth, "Thomas Hobbes and the Constituent Power of the People", in Mukherjee and Ramswami (ed.), *Great Western Thinkers.*

Raphael, D.D., *Hobbes : Marals and Politics,* George Allen and Unwin, London, 1977.

Subrata, Mukherjee and Sushila Ramswamy (ed.), *Great Western Political Thinkers,* Vol. 4, Deep and Deep, New delhi, 1993.

Thomas, Hobbes,*Leviathan,* in the English Works of Thomas Hobbes of Malmesbury, Sir William Molesworth (ed.), Vol. II, J. Bohn, London, 1836-1845; *Leviathan,* Richard Tuck (ed.), Cambridge Press, Cambridge, 1991 (Leviathan was first published in 1951).

Vincent, R.J., "The Hobbesian Tradition of Twentieth Century International Thought", *Millennium Journal of International Studies,* 1981.

IMMANUEL KANT

Andrew, Hurrell, Kant and Kantian Paradigm in International Relations", *Review of International Studies 16,* Printed in Great Britain, 1990.

Armstrong, A.C., "Kant's Philosophy of Peace and War", *Journal of Philosophy,* 1931.

Bourke, J., "Kant's Doctrine of Perpetual Peace", *Journal of Philosophy 32,* 1971.

Brian Porter, "Patterns of Thought and Practice : Martin Wight's International Theory", in Michael Donelan (ed.) *The Reason of States,* George Allen adn Unwin, London, 1980.

Dick Howard, "Kant's Political Theory : The Victue of his Vices", *Review of Metaphysics 34,* December 1980.

Forsyth, Sopar, M.G., and P. Savigear, *The Theory of International Relations : Selected Text From Gentil to Treitschke,* Allen and Unwin, London, 1970. This books contains a full text of "Perpetual Peace : A Philosophical Eassay", pp. 200-244.

Gallie W.B., "Wanted : A Philosophy of International Relations", *Political Studies*, XXVII, 1979.

Hans, Reiss (ed.), *Kant's Political Writings*, Cambridge, 1970. Original German texts are form Immanuel Kant, Werke in Sechs Banden, Wiesbaden, 1960.

Hastie, Edinburg, Kants Works, Vol. XII, total twelve columes were published for the firs time in English in 1970. Their two editions have come out but the greater authority is attributed to the second edition. The entire XII volumes are the translation of total VI volumes published by Ernst Casirer, Berlin in 1922-23 in German language. The original six volumes are actually published into twelve columes in English in 1970 but whose content and pagination is identical with that of the earlier six colume edition.

Hedley, Bull, "Society and Anarchy in Internatonal Relations", in Herbert Butterfield and Martin Wight (eds.), *Diplomatic Investigation*, Allen and Unwin, London, 1966; Martin "Wight and the Theory of International Relations", *British Journal of International Studies*, July 2, 1976; *Hobbes and International anarchy*, in Preston King (ed.), Vol. III, 1993.

Howard, Williams, *Kant's Political Philosphy*, Basic Blackwell, Oxford, London, 1983. See sp. Chapter 1. Man and History and chapter 10. Kant's plan for Internationoal Peace : The Highest Political Good and the highest moral good.

Immanual Kant, *The Metaphysics of Morals.* He deals, in this book with various aspects of international law as it then existed : the right to go to war, the laws in the war, the law after war and the laws of peace; *Idea for a Universal History with a Cosmo-plitan Purpose*, published in 1984. Kant introduces the idea of a federation in this book. He speaks of a man 'abandoning the lawless state of savagery and entering a federation of peoples in derive its security and rights not from his own power or its legal judgement but solely from this great federation; *On the Common Saying : This May be True in Theory but it does not Apply in Practice*, (pub. in 1793). In the book, Kant at first rejects the idea of a cosmopolitan commonwealth under a single head because of the danger of such a state leading to the most fearful despotism. Instead, he favours a lawful condition of federation with a commonly agreed international law. Yet only to pages later Kant's argument brings him back to the necessity of international law being based on coercion. He writes, "And there is not possible way of countering this (war and the will to subjugate others) except a state of international right, based on enforceable public laws to which every state must submit". Hence this study takes the position that Kant ultimately wanted to turn the union of pacific union into some form of universal political system able to enforce the law. Kant begins with an idea of limited federation gradually leading to the inauguration of an international state; *Perpetuate Peace, 1795.* In this book, Kant writes only about limited federation and how to bring about it and he is silent about, world government or the world authority with a power to enforce the law. He is at pains to underline the ned to maintain the independence of states and to uphold a strict principle of non-intervention. He was in search of a 'law governed external relationship' but rejects the idea of inventing a 'Leviathan'. He writes, "This federation does not aim to acquire any power like that of the state, but merely to preserve and secure the freedom of each state in itself along with that of all the other confederation states, although this does not mean that they need to submit to public laws and to a coercive power which enforces them as men do in the state of nature" (p. 104). It seems in Kant's mind, the exact nature of such a federation varics. Hence this work has taken a view which is taken by the Bull.

Martin Wight, "An Anatomy of Internatinoal Thought", *Review of Internatinal Studies*, July 3, 1987.

Michael Doyle, "Kant's Liberal Legacies and Foreign Affairs", *Philosophy and Publc Affairs*, 12, Summer, 1983.

Schuman Federick, "International Politics : Anarchy and Order", *World Society*, (ed.) Macgrow Hill, 1969.

Waltz, K.N., "Kant, Liberalism and War", *The American Political Science Review*, Vol. LVI, No. 2, June 1962.

Yirmiahu Jovel, *Kant and the Philosophy of History*, Princeton University Press, New Jersey, 1980.

HUGO GROTIUS

Alan James, *Sovereign Statehood: The basis of International Society*, London, 1986; *The Basis of International Order*, Oxford 1973.

Alexandrowicz Alendaner, "Grotius and India", *The Indian Year Book of International Affairs*, III, 1954.

Garnelius F. Murphy, Jr., "The Grotian Vision of World Order", *The American Journal of International Law*, Fred B. Rothman and Co., Vol. 76, 1982.

Clair Cutler, "The Grotian Tradition in International Relations", *Review of International Studies*, 16, Printed in Great Britain, 1990.

Gene M. Lyons, "The Study of International Relations in Great Britain : Further Connections", *World Politics*, 38, 1986.

Groom, A.J.R., (eds.), *International Relations : A Handbook of Current Theory*, Boulder, Colo., 1985.

Hedley Bull, "The Grotian Conception of Internatoinal Society", in H. Butterfield and Martin Wight (eds.), *Diplomatic Investigation*, pp. 51-73; "Martin Wight and the Theory of International Relations", *British Journal of International Studies, 2,* 1976; "The Importance of Grotius in the Study of International Relations", in Hedley Bull, Benddict, and Adam, (eds.), *Hugo Grotius and International Relations*, Glarendon Press, Oxford, 1992; "International Theory : The Case for a Classical Approach", in K. Knorr and J.N. Rosenau, (eds.), *Contemporary Approaches to International Politics*, Princeton, 1969.

Hidemi Suganami, "The Structure of Internationalism: An Anatomy of British Mainstream International Relations", *International Relations*, 7, 1983.

Hoffmann, S., "Hedley Bull and his Contribution to International Relatins", *International Affairs*, 62, 1986.

Hoslti, K.H., *The Dividing Discipline : Hegemony and Diversity in International Theory*, London, 1985; "Along the Road to International Theory", *International Journal*, 39, 1984. He notes that H. Bull's "Anarchical Society" is the most notable exposition on the Grotian concept that a society of states contains many bonds that brings stability and other that would not be found in a mere collection of sovereignties.

Hugo Grotius, *De Jure ac Pacis Libri Tres*, (JBP) first published in 1625 in Dutch. (Reference in this work is form Kelsey translation, Classics of International Law Edition 1925; cited as JBP books). Francis W. Kelsey, with the collaboration of Arthur E.R. Boak, Henry A. Sanders, Jesse S. Reeves, and Herbert F. Wright, OUP, Oxford, 1925, "Classics of International Law", New York, Oceana; Wildy and Sons, London, 1964.

Jones, Roy E., "The English School of International Relatons : A case of Closure", *Review of International Studies*, 7, 1981.

Lauterpacht H., "The Estern Values in International Relations", in Butterfield and Wight", *Diplomatic Investigations*; "An Anatomy of International Thought," *Review of Internatinoal Studies*, 13, 1987.

Michael Donelan, *Grotius and the Image of War*, Millennium, 12, 1983.

Sheila Grader, "The English School of International Relations : Evidence and Evaluation", *Review of International Studies*, 14, 1988.

Terry Nardin, *Law, Morality, and the Relations of States*, Princeton, New Jeresey, 1983.

GANDHI

Bhattacharya, Buddhadeva, *Evolution of the Political Philosophy of Gandhi*, Galcutta Book House, Calcutta, 1969.

Bhattacharya, N.C., *Gandhian Concept of State*, M.C. Sarkar and Sons, Calcutta, 1957.

Bondurant, Joan *Conquest of Violence*, Berkeley University of California Press, USA, 1965.

Bose Nirmal Kumar, *Selections From Gandhi*, Navjivan Ahmedabad, 1950; *Studies in Gandhism*, Nishan Publication, Calcutta, 1947.

clark, Grenwille, and Louis B. Sohm, *World Peace Through World Law*, Harvard University Press, Cambridge, 1960.

Dalla Dhirendra Moham *The Philosophy of Mahatma Gandhi*, Wisconsin, USA, 1953.

Datta, D.M., *The Philosophy of Mahatma Gandhi*, University of Wisconsin Press, Madison, 1944.

Desai Mahadeva, *The Gita According to Gandhi*, Navjivan, Ahmedabad, 1956.

Desai V.G., (trans. and ed.), *The Diary of Mahadev Desai*, Navjivan, Ahmedabad, 1953.

Diwakar, R.R. and Mahendra Agrawal, (ed.), *Gandho Marg*, 64 and 65, Vol. VI, No. 4 & 5, July-August 1984. This issue is specially on Peace Education.

Gandhi, M.K. *An Autobiography, My Experiments with Truth*, Navjivan, Ahmedabad, 1954; *Hind Swaraj*, Navjivan Ahmedabad, 1962; *Satyagraha in South Africa*, Navjivan, Ahmedabad, 1950; *Non-Violence in Peace and War*, Vol. I, Navjivan, Ahmedabad, 1948; *Delhi Diary*, Navjivan, Ahmedabad, 1948; *Unto This Last, A Paraphrase*, Navjivan, Ahmedabad, 1956; *Political and Natinal Life and Affairs*, V.B. Kher, (ed.), Navjivan, Ahmedabad, Vol. I,II,III, 1968.

Gangal, S.C., *The Gandhian Way to World Peace*, Vora and Co., Bombay, 1964.

Gene, Sharp, "Gandhi as a National Defence Strategist", *Gandhi Marg*, July 1970.

Ghosh, K.K., *Gandhi and World Peace and Understanding*, Modern Review, October, 1969.

Gregg, R.B., *The Power of Non-Violence*, Navjivan, Ahmedabad, 1948.

Guy de Mallac, *Gandhi's Seven Steps to Global Peace*, Ocean Tree Book, USA, 1989.

Nands, M.L., *Manifesto for a Peaceful World Order : A Gandhian Perspective*, Gandhi Bhavan, University of Delhi, 1983.

Handa, M.L., *The Existing World Order : Gandhian Interpretation.* November, 1981.

Hargopal G., *Gandhian World View : A Civil Liberty Perspective*, North-Eastern Hill University, Shillong, 1995.

Hingornai, Anand T., (ed.), *Towards Lasting Peace*, Bharatiya Vidya Bhavan, 1956.

James Williams, *The Moral Equivalent of War*, American Association for International Conciliation, 1910.

Kriplani, J.B. *Gandhian Approach to World Peace*, New Delhi.

Krishnamurti, Krishnamurti, Y.G., *Gandhi Era in World Politics*, Popular Book Depot, Bombay, 1943.

Mahendra Kumar, (ed.), *Non-Violence : Contemporary Issues and Challenges*, Gandhi Peace Foundation, New Delhi, 1994; *Non-Violence and the Science of International Relations.*

Mszumdar, Haridas, T., *Mahatma Gandhi's Philosophy of Soul Force*, The Modern Review, XCIX, February, 1956.

Mehrotra, S.R., "Gandhi and the British Commonwealth", *India Quarterly*, New Delhi, January-March 1961.

Mehta, G.L., *Gandhi as an Internationalist*, Indian Express, September 2, 1969.

Misrs, K.P., and Gangal S.C. (ed.), *Gandhi and the Contemporary World*, (Studies in Peace and War), Chanakya Publication, Delhi, 1981.

Murty, K.S. and A.C. Bouquet, *Studies in Problems of Peace*, Asia Publishing, Bombay, 1960.

Naess arne, *Gandhi and Nuclear Age*, Totowa, Bedminister Press, N.J., 1965; "A Systemization of Gandhian Ethics of Conflict Resolution", *Journal of Conflict Resolution*, II, June 1958.

Nageshwar Prasad (ed.) *Hind Swaraj : A Fresh Look*, Gandhi Peace Foundatin, New Delhi, 1985.

Nanda, B.R., *Mahatna Gandhi : A Biography*, Allen adn Unwin, London, 1959.

Nanda, B.R., *Gandhi : Pan Islamism, Imperialism and Natonalism in India*, Oxford University Press, Bombay, 1989.

Narayan, Shriman, *Towards a Non-Violent Social Order*, Yojna, Delhi, October 1969.

Oberg, Jan. "Cosmology, Peace and World Order", *Gandhi Marg*, July 1987.

Parmeshwaran, (ed.), *Gandhi, Lohia and Deendayal*, Deendayal Research Institute, New Delhi, 1978.

Patil, V.T. (ed.), *Studies on Gandhi*, Sterling Publication, New Delhi, 1984; *Problems and Issues in Gandhism*, Inter-India Publication, New Delhi, 1990.

Paul, F. Power, *Gandhi on World Affairs*, George Allen and Unwin Ltd., London 1961.

Puri, Rashmi-Sudha, *Gandhi on War and Peace*, Praeger, New Yorn, 1987; "Gandhi and the Second World War", *Indian Journal of Political Science*, 38, January, 1977.

Richards, *Philosophy of Gandhi : A Study of his Basic Ideas*, Curson Press, London, 1982.

Roy Chudhury, P.C., *Gandhi and International Politics*, Navjivan, Ahmedabad, 1970, *Gandhiji and International Politics*, Navjivan, Ahmedabad, 1970; *Gandhiji and Internationlist Politics*, Navjivan, Ahmedabad, 1970.

Sant Ram Mandal, *Gandhi and World Peace*, Loss Angles, April 1952.

Sethi, J.D., *Intrnational Economic Disorder and a Gandhian Solution*, (A theory of Economic Darvinism), Vikas Publishing House, New Delhi, 1990.

Sharma, K.N, (ed.), *Peaçe Technology and Development*, Rawat Publications, Jaipur, 1990.

Sharp, Gene, *Gandhi Wields the Weapon of Moral Power*, Navjivan, Ahmedabad, 1960.

Shridharani Krishanlal, *War Without Violence*, Bharatiya Vidya Bhavan, Bombay, 1962.

Singh, R., *Gandhi and the Modern World*, Classical Publication Co., New Delhi, 1988.

Sunita Kataria, *Gandhi's Reactions to World Affairs*, Kanishka Publication, Delhi, 1990.

Tikekar, Indu B., *Integral Revolution*. An Analytical Study of Gandhian Thought. Sarva Seva Sangh Prakashan, Varanasi, 1970.

JAWAHARLAL NEHRU

Arnold, Toynbee, *One World and India*, Indian Council for Cultural Relations, New Delhi, 1960.

Attar, Chand, *Henru on World Order*, Anmol Publication, New Delhi, 1992.

Chester, Bowles, *The New Dimensions of Peace*, Harper and Brothers, New York, 1955.

Das, M.N., *The Political Philosophy of Jawaharlal Nehru*, George Alen and Unwin, London, 1961.

Durga, *India : From Curzon to Nehru and After*, Collins, London, 1969.

Frank, R. Morses, *Jawaharlal Nehru : A Biography*, Macmillan, New York, 1956; *Nehru : Sunlight and Shadow*, Jaico Publishing House, Bombay, 1964.

Ganesh, Prasad, "Nehru and Nationalism", *Mainstream*, May 29, 1971.

Gayon, Naba, K., *Jawaharlal Nehru and the National Idea*, Patriot, New Delhi, November 7, 1980.

Gopal Sarvepalli (ed.), *Jawaharlal Nehru : An Anthology*, Oxford University Press, New delhi, 1980.

Haksar, P.N., *Nehru's Vision of Peace and Security in Nuclear Age*, Patriot, New Delhi, 1987.

Jayaramu, P.S., *Nehru's approach to Security : India's National Security and Foreign Policy*, New Delhi, 1987.

Kamath, "Nehru's Non-Alignment and the West", *Times of India*, Bombay, November 14, 1988.

Khan, Rasheeduddin, "Nehru's Vision of Peace and Security", *Mainstream*, Republic Day, 1987.

Menon, P. Gopinath, "Jawaharlal Nehru and Collective Security in Asia", *Soviet Review*, 25 May 1974.

Menon, K.P.S., *Jawaharlal Nehru : Apostle of Peace*, Amrita Bazar Patrika, 14 November, 1978.

Michael, Brecher, *Nehru : A Political Biography*.

Nanda, B.R., (ed.), *Indian Foreign Policy - The Nehru Years*, Vikas Publishing, New Delhi, 1976.

Narasimha Char, K.T., *The Quintessence of Nehru*, George Allen and Unwin, London, 1961.

Nehru, Jawaharla, *An Autobiography*, Badley Head, London, 1936; *The Discovery of India*, Signet Press, Calcutta, 1946; *Mahatma Gandhi*, Signet Press, Calcutta, 1949; *Independence and After : Government of India*, Publication Division, New Delhi, 1949; *Freedom From Fear, Reflections on the Personality and Teachings of Gandhi*, Government of India, Publication Division , New Delhi, 1960; *A Bunch of Old Letters*, Asia Publishing, London, 1960; "Problems of Peace", *New Wave*,, 20 December 1987; "How Deep is Our Nationalism", *New Wave*, March 20, 1982; "Nationalism and Mass Struggle in India", *Labour Monthly*, August 20, 1938.

Pal, K.C., "The Panchshila and World Pace", *Modern Reivew*, February 1956.

Patil, V.T., (ed.), *Studies on Nehru*, Sterling Publication, New Delhi, 1987; *Explorations in Nehruvian Thought*, Inter-India Publication, New

Delhi, 1992; *Nationalism, freedom and Socialism, Nehru and the Freedom Movement*, Sterling, New Delhi, 1977.

Rafiq Zakaria, (ed.), "A Study of Nehru", *Times of India*, 1960. This book is a commemorative value brought out on the occasion of seventieth birth anniverssary of Jawaharlal Nehru. Many outstanding scholars and eminent persons have contributed to this volume.

Ramchandram, G., *Nehru and World Peace*, Radiant Publication, New Delhi, 1990.

Rana, A.P., *The Imperatives of Nonalignment : A Conceptual Study of India's Foreign Policy Strategy in the Nehru Period*, Macmillan, New Delhi, 1976 and 1979.

Rifaquat, Ali, S., "Nehru : Man of Peace", *Mainstream*, 29 May 1971.

Singh, J.N., *Apostle of Peace*, National Herald, 14 November 1980.

Vinkatasubbaiah, P., "Nehru's Nationalism and Internationalism", *India Nation*, November 14, 1986.

Vishnu, Dutt, *Gandhi, Nehru and the Challenge*, Abinav Publications, New Delhi, 1979.

Werner, Levi, *Free India in Asia*, University of Minnesota Press, Minneapolis, 1954.

Williard Range, *Jawaharlal Nehru's World View : A Theory of International Relations*, University of Georgia Press, Athens, 1961.

RAM MANOHAR LOHIA

Arumugam (M), *Socialist Thought in India : The Contribution of Ram Manohar Lohia*, Sterling Publishers, New Delhi, 1978.

Canesh Mantri (ed.), *Samata Ka Darshan (Lohia, Ak Vishleshan)*, Samata Adhayana Kendra, Goregao, Bombay.

Cyan Chand, "On Reading Lohia's Sheel of History, *Mankind*, Vol. 1, No. 5, December 1956.

Indumati Kelkar, *Lohia, Sindhant Aur Karm*, Navhind Prakashan, Hyderabad, 1971.

Krishna Nand Thakur, *Dr. R. Lohia Ke Aarthic*, Rajnitik Anvam Samajik Vichar, S. Chand and Co., Ltd., New Delhi.

Kurian, P.V., "Ideas for New-Civilization", *Mankind*, May 1968.

K. Gopinath Pillai, *Political Philosophy of Ram Manohar Lohia : Alternative Development Perception*, Deep and Deep, New Delhi, 1994.

Lohia, Ram Manohar, *Fragments of a World Mind*, Maitrayani, Calcutta, 1953; *sheet of History*, R. Lohia Samata Vidyalaya, Hyderabad, 1974; *Vill to Power and other Writings*, Navhind Prakasha, Hyderabad,

1956; *Third Camp in World Affairs*, Madhu Limaye for the Socialist Party, National House, Bombay, 1960; *A Policy for the War and Peace in the Himalayas*, George Fernandes, Bombay; *Foreign Policy*, P.C., Dwadash Shreni and Co (P) Ltd., aligarh; *India, China and Northern Frontiers*, Novhind Prakashan, Hyderabad, 1964; *Marx, Gandhi and Socialism*, R. Lohia Samata Vidyalaya, 1978; *Indians in Foreign Lands*, All India Congress Committee, Allahabad, 1938; *Action in Goa*, August Publication House, 1947; *Guilty Men of India's Partition*, R. Lohia Samata Vidyalaya, 1970; "Some Reflections on Internationalism", *Mankind*, Vol. I, No. 2, September 1956; "Meaning of Equality", *Mankind*, Vol. 1, No. 4, November 1956; "Defects of Political Parties in India", *Mankind*, Vol. 1, No. 7, February 1957; "Questions Before the Party and the Nation", *Mankind*, Vol. 2, No. 9, April 1958; "Some Problems of Nation-Building", *Mankind*, (Press Conference in Hyderabad on January 16, 1958) Vol. II, No. 7, February 1958; "Squint Eyed Historian and Cosy Intellectuals", *Mankind*, Vol. 3, No. 1, August 1958; "Gandhism and Socialism", *Mankind*, Vol. 4, No. 8, March 1960; "International Landmarks", *Congress Socialist*, Vol. 1, No. 52, December 26, 1936; "The Collapse of International Morality", *Congress Socialist* Vol. 3, No. 9, February 1938; "International Balance Sheet", *Congress Socialist* Vol. 3, No. 10, March 5, 1938; "The Dilemma of an Anti-Imperialist", *Congress Socialist* Vol. 3, No. 14, April 2, 1938; "The Conquest of Violence", *Congress Socialist*, Vol. 3, No. 15, April 9, 1938; "Jawahar Must Answer", *Congress Socialist*, Col. 3, No. 18, April 30, 1938; "India and Britain's War", *Congress Socialist*, Vol. 3, No. 40, October 2, 1938; "War Resister", *Congress Socialist* Vol. 4, No. 14, April 2, 1939; "India and the International Situation", *Janata*, The Socialist Approach, March 23, 1947; "Communism Europe's Weapon Against Asia", *Janata*, Vo. 3, No. 36, September 26, 1948; "Introduction to Foundation for World Government", *Janata*, Vol. 5, No. 16, May 7, 1950; "Third Force and World View: Report on Foreign Affairs", *Janata*, Vol. 5, No. 27, July 23, 1950; "Third Force Alone Can Avert War", *Janata*, Vol. 5, No. 48, December 17, 1950; "Neutralism in International Politics", *Janata*, Vol. 6, No. 3, February 11, 1951; "Reinforcing a Constructive Foreign Policy of Building the New World", *Janata*, Vol. 6, No. 19, June 3, 1951; "Equality of all National Essential for World Peace", *Janata*, Vol. 6, No. 28, August 12, 1951; "All Excitement and No Accomplishment that is Nehru's Foreign Policy", *Janata*, Vol. 6, No. 37, October 14, 1951; "Joint Statement by Dr. Lohia and Professor Diumblatte", *Janata*, Vol. 6, No. 46, December 16, 1951; "A Five Point Foreign Policy for India", *Janata*, Vol. 6, No. 47, December 23, 1951; "The Driving Forces of History : Dr. Lohia's Analysis", *Janata*, Vol. 7, No. 1, July 20, 1952; "The Arab World is Potentially of the Third Camp", *Janata*, Vol. 7, No. 8, September 7, 1952; "India's Foreign Policy", *Janata*, Vol. 9, No. 2, January 31, 1954; "Theory of Equidistance", *Janata*, Vol. 9, No. 11, April 4, 1957; "The UNO Charter", *Janata*, Vol. 9, No. 14, April 25, 1954; "Revolution History and Fable", *Janata*, Vol. 9, No. 15, May 1, 1954; "Imperialism; Communist and Capitalist", *Janata*, Vol. 9, No. 22, June 20, 1954; "India and Britain's War : Way to Combat Design of Imperialist", *National Herald*, January 12, 1939; "To Hell With Arms", *National Herald*, November 10, 1939; "Non-violence, The Salvation Statement before the Court", *Hational Herald*, July 17, 1940.

Majumdar, R.C., "On Reading Lohia's Statement", *Mankind*, Vol. 2, No. 3, Nagpur, October, 1957.

Mehrotra, (N.C.), *Socialist Thought in India : The Contribution of Ram Manohar Lohia*, Sterling Publishers, New Delhi, 1978.

Mishra, Cirish, *Ram Manohar Lohia : The Man and His Ism*, Eastern Publication, New Delhi, 1992.

Mitra Roma, *Lohia Through Letters*, Roma Mitra Publication, New Delhi.

Onkar, Sharad, *Lohia*, Lucknow Prakashan Kendra, Lucknow, 1972.

Rajendra Mohan Bhatnagar, *Bharat Ke Gaurav Nirbhik Neta Tatha Krantikari Vicharak Ki Jivani*, Kitab Ghar Publication, Delhi, 1978, *Lohiaka Jivan Darshan*, Kitab Ghar, Delhi, 1979; *Samagra Lohia*, Kitab Ghar, Delhi, 1982.

Shibte Muhmmad Naqui, *Dr. Lohia : Aik Zalak (Urdu)*, Akvarpur, Faizabad.

Varma Rajnikant, *Lohia*, Rashmi Prakashan, Allahabad, 1969.

Wofford Jr., Harris, *Lohia and america Meet*, Snehlata Ram Reddy, Madras, 1961; "Gandhian Socialism and the Third Camp", *Mankind*, August-September, 1961.

Yatindra Nath Sharma, *Dr. Lohia : Arth Darshan*, Chitra Prakashan, Kanpur, 1979.

ENCYCLOPEDIA - PERIODICALS AND JOURNALS

1. Sills, I. David (ed.), *International Encyclopaedia of Social Science*, London, 1969.

2. Edwards Paul, (ed. in Chief), *Encyclopaedia of Philosophy*, Vol. CI, New York, 1967.
3. *Gandhi Marg*, New Delhi.
4. *Congress Socialist*, Calcutta.
5. *Mankind*, Hyderabad.
6. *Janata*, Bombay.
7. *Harijan*, Poona (1944-40), Madras (1934-35).
8. *Young India*, Ahmedabad, 1919-22.

□□□

INDEX

***